CRAPS

TAKE THE MONEY AND RUN

by
Henry J. Tamburin

Research Services Unlimited
P.O. Box 19727
Greensboro, NC 27419

CRAPS: TAKE THE MONEY AND RUN
Copyright© 1995 by Henry J.Tamburin

Address all inquiries to the publisher:
Research Services Unlimited
P.O. Box 19727
Greensboro, NC 27419

Manufactured in the United States of America

ISBN: 0-912177-10-1
Library of Congress catalog card number: 95-67044

Eighth Printing, April 2003

The material contained in this book is intended to inform and educate the reader and in no way represents an inducement to gamble legally or illegally.

Preface

My goal in writing this book is to teach you how to play casino craps in a way that will significantly improve your chances of winning. You will learn a playing and betting strategy that involves taking advantage of the multiple odds now being offered by casinos throughout the country.

Although the casino has the long term advantage over all craps players, over the short term it is possible to win. What it takes is the knowledge of which bets to make, when to increase your bets, and most importantly, when to quit.

Part of the contents of this book first appeared in *Henry Tamburin on Casino Gambling* and in course notes and articles I have written over the years on casino craps. All of this material was expanded, revised, and brought up to date to form the contents of this book.

I have been playing craps in casinos throughout the country for 25 years and know first hand that to be a winning craps player you must first learn how to reduce the casino's edge to as low as possible. Couple this with a sound money management plan and the discipline to quit when you are ahead ("take the money and run") and you'll have a strategy for craps that will allow you to enjoy many winning sessions.

This book assumes you have never played craps

before and Chapters 1 through 3 give an explanation of the craps layout, the functions of the dealer, the mechanics of how the game is played, and a review of the dice odds. A schematic of a typical craps layout is included in Chapter 2 which you can refer back to as each of the different bets are discussed.

Chapter 4 contains an explanation of the basic playing rules for casino craps. Even if you've never played the game before, you will readily learn the basics.

Chapters 5 through 11 explain in detail all of the different types of bets that are available to craps players. A summary of the casino's advantage for all of these bets is contained in Chapter 12.

My recommended winning techniques are contained in Chapters 13 and 14. Here you will learn the *Increased Odds* system for minimizing the casino's advantage and escalating your bets for maximum profits when the rolls of the dice are going your way.

Most craps players are confused as to which bets can be removed from the layout and which can not. Chapter 15 clarifies this point to eliminate the confusion.

Hedge betting or insurance betting has become the "in thing" to do at the craps tables. While some Hedge betting can be good, most others are not. Chapter 16 explains this concept with a recommended Hedge betting strategy for the conservative player.

Chapter 17 answers the question "if multiple odds is such a good deal for the player, why do casinos offer it?" The answer may surprise you.

A modified version of casino craps has debuted in a Mississippi casino. It's called "Never Ever Craps" and is touted as a better game for the player. But is it? Read Chapter 18 and find out.

Casinos have also recently introduced an electronic version of craps played on a rectangular layout without dealers. Called "Live Video Craps," it offers the beginner the opportunity to play craps at lower stakes than the regular table games. However, as you'll read in Chapter 19, the rules strongly favor the casino.

Chapter 20 contains a collection of craps systems that I have used over the years. These systems "tell" the player which bets to make and when to increase the bet size. As long as a system of play avoids high percentage bets, there is nothing wrong with using them.

Craps dealers can often be helpful to novice players. In Chapter 21 you'll learn how to tip or toke them for their services.

Craps tournaments are growing in popularity because they offer the average player an opportunity to win thousands of dollars. I suggest some tournament strategies in Chapter 22 based upon my tournament experiences.

The last chapter (23) describes the playing attitudes and styles of the typical losing "dumb" craps player. This unfortunate player is often courted by the casinos because of his potential to lose big. Craps dealers love him because he usually tips very frequently and the less informed players seem to envy his style of play.

I would like to thank my wife, Linda, for helping me proof read the manuscript, Chris Schneider for typesetting the book and Ben Jordan for the cover design. I also must thank Gil Stead and the late Sam Grafstein who taught me early on what it takes to be a winning craps player.

I'd be most interested in hearing from the readers of this book (pros and cons) so that I can continually improve it. Please send your written comments to the publisher (Research Services Unlimited), my attention.

Craps is one of the most exciting casino games where it's possible to win a lot of money in a very short period of time. I wish you much success in becoming a winning player who learns how to *take the money and run.*

Henry J. Tamburin

TABLE OF CONTENTS

Preface iii

Chapters
1   Why Play? 1
2   The Layout 5
3   Dice Odds 9
4   Beginner Basics 13
5   Odds Bet 17
6   Come and Don't Come Bets 25
7   Place Bets 33
8   Buy and Lay Bets 39
9   Field Bet 43
10 Big 6 and 8 47
11 Proposition Bets 51
12 Casino Advantage 57
13 Winning Strategies for the Right Bettor 61
14 Winning Strategies for the Wrong Bettor 71
15 Removing Bets from the Layout 77
16 Hedge Betting 81
17 Multiple Odds Revisited 85
18 Never Ever Craps 89
19 Live Video Craps 93
20 Systems 97
21 Dealer Tipping 107
22 Craps Tournaments 109
23 The Dumb Craps Player 113
    Glossary 115
    Suggested Reading 121
    Index 123

1

Why Play?

"Winner seven, take the don't pass and pay the pass line." "Same shooter coming out, craps yo'leven, two, three or seven." "Five no field five, take the field, put the comes on five, the don't comes behind the five."

Craps is the fastest and most exciting casino game that offers the player the best wager in the house. However, most novice players are reluctant to play because they are confused by the multitude of bets possible and the fast action on the table. In fact, 80% of these bets are "poor" bets which have a very high casino edge. The key to winning is to confine your play to those 20% wagers with the lowest casino edge and to learn when to quit.

Some of the advantages the game of craps offers to a player is the following:

1. A player can win the most amount of money in the shortest possible time.

2. There are no difficult playing strategies to remember (compared to blackjack).

1

3.   If a player is winning big, the casinos can't stop him or her from playing. In fact all they can do is reluctantly pay off the winning bets.

4.   Craps is a personal game...a player feels more involved because he or she initiates the action (by rolling the dice) that results in their win or loss.

5.   There is a tremendous camaraderie at the craps table...mostly everyone roots and cheers for the shooter (or roller) to win.

6.   The game offers the intelligent player a chance to make a wager with less than 1% casino advantage.

From the casino standpoint, craps is a money maker. Each and every craps table in a major Las Vegas strip casino is expected to generate a one million dollar per year profit. And these are the reasons for the large casino profits.

1.   Most of the so called knowledgeable players really don't understand the odds and probabilities of the various craps wagers. They'll scoff at the roulette player for playing such a "dumb" game yet these same players won't hesitate to make a field or proposition bet with equal or worse odds.

2.   Craps is the domain of the high rollers. The big bettor loves a game where money action predominates. Craps offers a game where a player can wager money on several bets after each dice roll. And in the heat of the battle, in the excitement of the table, the player usually spreads his money "all over the table" hoping for the quick kill. In the majority of cases however, it's the player that gets wiped out.

Even though the casino enjoys the advantage over the player on every craps wager, it still is possible to win over the short term. All it takes is:

1. Knowledge of the odds and probabilities.

2. Knowledge of which bets to make and which to avoid.

3. Knowledge of how to bet and when to quit.

So let's begin to gain this knowledge.

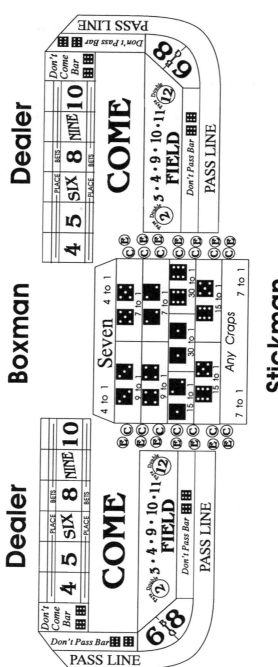

2

The Layout

Before we can discuss winning strategies, it is important that you understand the fundamentals of the casino game of craps. Let's start with the craps table itself. If you've never seen one, it's the size of a billiard table and printed on the felt surface of the table is the layout for making bets.

There are three sections to the layout (see p. 4). Two of them are identical and mirror images separated by a center portion. Players stand at the perimeter of the table and either place their chips directly on the bet they wish to make on the layout or they place their chips on the layout and instruct the dealer where to place the bet.

Casino Staff

The casino uses four to five employees to operate the game. The tasks of these employees are:

Dealers - There are two, one on each end of the table who handle the betting action, pay winning bets and collect losing bets.

5

Stickperson - He or she stands in the middle of the table on the players side in front of the center betting area of the layout. The stickperson controls the pace of the game, is in charge of the dice and places bets for players in the center of the layout. The term stickperson comes from the fact that they use a long hooked stick to maneuver the dice about the table.

Boxperson - He or she is the boss of the table. This individual is seated opposite the stickperson and keeps tabs on everything that goes on - the dice, players, dealers, payoffs and so forth. This person is also responsible for the casino bank, which sets in front of him or her, and is carefully monitored. All disputes are handled by this person.

Craps tables are arranged in an area of the casino floor that is known as the "craps pit." The entire pit, which may comprise several craps tables, is supervised by the pitboss. Reporting directly to the pitboss are floorpersons, who are assigned to specific tables. Floorpersons observe the games to be sure no cheating occurs, and in particular, they keep tabs of players who have asked to be rated. They also handle giving credit to players and receive assistance from the pit bookkeeper.

Casino Chips

In the majority of gambling jurisdictions, cash can not be used to bet at the table. Before you begin to play you must give your money to the dealer who will exchange it for casino chips. Never hand money to a dealer; always drop it on the table for him or her to pick up.

Before you play, be certain to read the placard located on the table by each dealer which describes the minimum and maximum bets allowed for that particular craps table. At the end of a playing session, a player can leave the table with his or her chips which can be exchanged for currency at the casino cashier cage.

Running all around the top of the craps table you'll find grooved rails to hold your chips while you play. Be careful to keep an eye on your chips. There are a minority of unscrupulous players who use the excitement of the tables to swipe a chip or two from unsuspecting players.

You are responsible for your bets on the layout. Often times there will be many chips from different players on the layout. On some bets, the dealer will pay off a winning wager by simply placing the winning chips next to the original bet. It's your responsibility to pick up those chips. I guarantee you, that if you don't, someone else will.

Often times you will need to make a bet of a certain amount such as $6 to get a correct payoff (more about this later). If you don't have exactly $6 worth of chips, you can just place, for example, two five dollar chips on the bet and tell the dealer you are waging $6. The dealer will make the correct "change", leave $6 on the layout and return $4 to you.

Always keep in mind that dealers are not allowed to physically hand you chips nor are you suppose to hand cash to a dealer. Winning payoffs are always placed by the dealer on the layout next to the original bet or the dealer will place the chips directly in front of the player to pick up.

Now is a good time to mention the free craps lessons that most casinos offer to novice players. This is an excellent way to "get the lay of the land," and a good review of the craps layout and functions of the dealers. Simply ask any casino supervisor when those lessons occur.

Now that you understand the craps layout, we need to review a little about the mathematics of craps. This is not heavy math, just basic dice odds which are important to know to better understand the game.

3

Dice Odds

In order to thoroughly understand the game of craps, it is important to understand the dice probabilities.

The game of craps is played with two dice. Each die is a six sided cube and each side has imprinted one to six dots known as pips. Casino dice measure about three-quarters of an inch on each side, are transparent, usually red and have the casino's name or logo imprinted on them. Casino dice are also coded to be certain that no other dice can be introduced into the game. It is the boxperson's job to keep track of the dice and examine them from time to time (especially if they are thrown off the table). Next time you watch a craps game, also observe the stickperson twirl the dice on the table with the stick between dice rolls. Reason? To be certain that each die has all of the six numbers (1 through 6) on them and the positions of the numbers is such that the number on the top and bottom of the die total seven (one is opposite six; two is opposite five; and three is opposite four). All of these checks are to ensure the players a fair game.

When a pair of dice are rolled, there are eleven

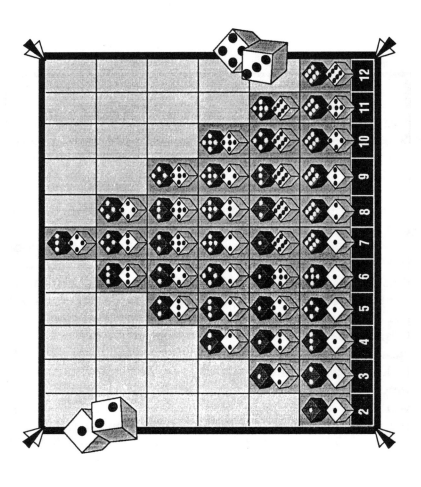

different totals which can appear. These are the totals 2 through 12. More importantly, these eleven different numbers can be rolled in 36 different combinations (see page 10).

By referring to the diagram on page 10, it is possible to calculate the odds for rolling any particular number. For example, what are the odds of anyone picking up a pair of dice in any casino in the world and rolling a seven? Examining the diagram we find that a seven can be rolled in only six out of the possible thirty six dice combinations. Thus the odds of rolling a seven are 30 to 6 (thirty combinations yield a non-seven; only six yield a seven). Dividing by five yields the common "odds against seven" of 5 to 1.

Let us suppose we want to calculate the odds against rolling a four before a seven. A quick look at the dice diagram reveals that a four can be rolled in three different combinations and a seven in six different combinations. Hence the odds of rolling a four before a seven are 6 to 3 or 2 to 1.

If you are new to the game of craps, study the diagram well because the entire game of craps including the advantage or disadvantage a player may have by making a bet, and the amounts paid on winning bets is based upon these dice odds.

The most important odds for the bets that you will be making are the odds of throwing one of the numbers listed at the top of the layout (numbers 4, 5, 6, 8, 9, 10) vs. throwing a 7. These odds are:

Number	Odds of Making
4, 10	2 to 1
5, 9	3 to 2
6, 8	6 to 5

The easiest way to learn the above is to remember the outside numbers (4, 10) have 2 to 1 odds, the inside numbers (5, 9) are 3 to 2, and the 6, 8 have 6 to 5 odds.

Etiquette

Craps players, especially veteran players, tend to be very superstitious and they believe that certain events, if they occur at the craps table, will cause them to lose. These "myths" are part of the culture of craps and it's important you are aware of them so you don't "upset" veteran players. Just keep in mind the following:

1. Don't dangle your hands over the rails, especially when someone is ready to throw the dice (the superstition is that if the dice hit a player's hand, a seven is sure to be rolled). Be especially careful when you pick up your chips after buying in. The stickperson will keep the dice in the center of the table until players complete making their bets. Once the dealer slides the dice to a player that's your cue to keep your hands up because a player will be throwing the dice.

2. Don't mention the number "seven" at the craps table. This is bad etiquette and will definitely upset players. The reason is because the majority of players will lose when a seven is rolled after a point is established. It is an unmentionable number at the craps table. Since the number 11 can sound like the number 7, craps players and dealers refer to the number 11 as yo'leven.

3. If you toss the dice and accidently one (or both) dice leave the table, shout out "same dice." Again veteran craps players believe if new dice are put into play it's the kiss of death and will cause them to lose.

4. If someone is having a good roll, don't talk to that person. Veteran players believe that if you break the concentration of a shooter, he/she will surely throw a seven.

Now we are ready to learn the basics of craps, namely betting on the pass line.

4

Beginner Basics

To participate in craps, you must first convert your cash into casino chips or checks. To do this at the craps table, you simply place your money down on the table prior to a dice roll, get the dealer's attention and ask "chips please." The dealer will convert your cash into chips and place the chips in front of you on the layout. Bend down, pick up your chips and place them in the grooved rails in front of you. You're now ready to bet.

One of the better bets to make is a wager on the pass line. To do so, you simply place your chips on the area of the layout marked pass line. (It runs all around the outside of the layout - see page 4). You win or lose the bet as follows.

If the shooter or dice roller throws a 7 or 11 (naturals) on the first roll of the dice in a new game (known as the come-out roll) you win. If instead, the number thrown is 2, 3 or 12 (craps numbers) you lose.

Any other number rolled - 4, 5, 6, 8, 9, 10 - establishes the shooter's point. To win your bet, the shooter must pick up the dice and continue to throw them (these rolls are known as point rolls) until he or she either rolls the point number before rolling a seven - in which case you win - or rolls a seven before the point number - in which case you lose.

Let's try some examples. You make a bet on the pass line and the come-out roll is a 4. The next rolls are 3, 11, 6, 7. You lose because the 7 was rolled before the point number 4 repeated.

Suppose the dice were thrown in the following sequence: 11, 2, 6, 8, 7, 7, 5, 6, 7. The first throw (come-out roll) wins because the roll was 11. The second come-out roll, 2 results in a loss. The third come-out roll established 6 as the point. The next point roll, 8 leads to no decision. The next point roll, 7 results in a loss since the 7 appeared before the 6 point number repeated. The next come-out roll is a 7 and we win. The next come-out is a 5 which establishes the shooter's point. The point roll 6 results in no decision. The point roll 7 results in a loss.

In the event you win a pass line bet, the payoff is 1 to 1 (if you bet $5 you win $5). You must also remember that the pass line bet is a contract bet. What this means is that once you put your chips on the pass line, you are not permitted, once a point is established, to either add more chips, remove some chips, or remove the bet from the layout. The bet stays as is until it either wins or loses.

Betting on the pass line is known as betting with the shooter or betting right. The majority of craps players bet in this manner because they are optimistic and are rooting for the shooter to make his or her point. There are however a number of players who bet "against the dice" or bet wrong. To do this, you would bet on the don't pass line (see layout for location of don't pass betting area).

If you wager on the don't pass and the come-out roll is either 2 or 3 you win. If instead, it's a 7 or 11, you lose. If a point number is established, you win if the seven repeats before the point number and lose if the point number repeats before the seven. The winning payoff is again 1 to 1.

As you can see, the rules for winning or losing on the don't pass are opposite to the pass line with one exception. If a 12 is thrown on the come-out roll, the pass line bet loses but the don't pass bet is a push or tie. The latter is done to prevent the don't pass bettor from having the advantage over the casino. By "barring the 12," on the come-out roll, the casino's advantage over the player is virtually the same for the pass or don't pass. Mathematically, this advantage is about 1.4% or in terms of dollars and cents the player stands to lose on the average about seven cents per five dollar bet.

Here are some additional pointers regarding table etiquette and game rules.

Each craps table has a minimum bet requirement which is posted on a sign next to the dealers on either end of the table. In most casinos these signs are color coded. A white sign indicates $2 or $3 minimum; red indicates $5 table minimum; yellow indicates a $10 minimum bet and green indicates a $25 minimum bet requirement. Maximum bets vary from casino to casino with most offering up to $1000 or $2000.

Some casinos, such as Binion's Horseshoe in Las Vegas, will book very large bets, including a million dollar bet, upon request.

You are responsible for making your pass or don't pass bet and when you win, you must pick up your chips (the dealers won't hand you your winnings).

Always place your bet before the dice are thrown. If you don't, the bet may be disallowed. As mentioned earlier, many craps players are superstitious and believe that if the dice hit a player's hands, it's bad luck. So never let your hands get in the way of the dice as they are thrown (keep them up - don't dangle them).

Whenever a player throws a seven on a point roll this is known as "sevening out" and the shooter must relinquish the dice to the next player. The dice pass around the table with everyone having an opportunity to throw them.

However, you don't have to throw the dice if you don't want to - simply tell the dealer this when offered the dice and they will give them to the next player. If you do decide to roll the dice, then you must as a shooter, make either a bet on the pass line or the opposite don't pass. Always try to toss the dice (like tossing a cup of water) so that the dice rebound against the back wall at the opposite end of the table (this ensures a random roll). If you don't do this the dealers may disallow the roll (you'll hear "no roll") and you'll be chastised.

Also, you should always keep the dice in view of the boxperson at all times and use one hand to pick them up and throw them (don't for example, pick up the dice and shake them in your hand under the table).

Many players enjoy craps because it's the one casino game where you can scream and shout and let it all hang out. You will find a camaraderie at the craps table that you don't find at the other games. Everyone is shouting and rooting for the shooter to make his point. And many players like the feeling of being able to initiate the action (by throwing the dice) which determines whether they win or lose.

5

Odds Bet

The very best bet in the casino happens to be located on the craps table. Not to surprising is the fact that this best bet isn't even marked on the layout and no one will tell you about it if you don't ask. The best bet is called the odds bet.

The reason that the odds bet is the best bet is that this is the only casino bet in which the house doesn't enjoy a percent edge or advantage over the player. Thus the casino payoff on the winning odds bet is equal to the risk involved in making that bet and hence the casino's advantage over the player is zero. Except for the game of blackjack played skillfully, this is the lowest casino advantage bet available to the player.

The odds bet can only be made after you make an initial pass line bet. In other words the odds bet is not an independent bet which can solely be made on the craps table, but must be made in conjunction with the pass line bet (or as you'll learn shortly, the don't pass, come and don't come bets). The effect of making this odds bet (with 0 casino advantage) is that the normal pass line casino advantage of 1.41% is reduced to a low 0.85%. This means over the long run you can expect a return of $99.15 for every $100 wagered (compare this to the slot machine player whose expectation is only about $90-$95 for every $100 wagered).

So how do you make this best bet which isn't even marked on the craps layout? It's actually quite simple to do and goes like this.

First you must make a wager on the pass line at the start of a new dice roll. Immediately after the dice shooter establishes a point, you physically take an amount of chips equal in value to the original pass line bet and place these chips (your odds bet) directly behind your original pass line bet. And if you've never done this before and feel uneasy, ask the dealer to help you because this is part of their job.

You will now have on the layout a wager on the pass line and an equivalent wager behind this bet (the odds bet or as it's sometimes referred to, the backline bet). If the shooter makes his point, start jumping for joy, because the winning payoffs will be 1 to 1 on the pass line bet and more important, you will be paid *greater* than 1 to 1 on the winning odds bet. The exact payoff depends on the point number that was established by the shooter. If the shooter's point was 4 or 10 then your odds payoff will be 2 to 1; if the point was 5 or 9 it's a 3 to 2 payoff and the payoff for a 6 or 8 point is 6 to 5. Translating these payoffs in terms of dollars means that if you wager, for example $10 on the pass line with a $10 odds bet, you receive $10 in payoff for the winning pass line bet and a $20 odds payoff if the point was 4 or 10, $15 for point 5 or 9 and $12 for point 6 or 8. These 2 to 1, 3 to 2 and 6 to 5 payoffs are equal to the probability of the shooter making his or her point which accounts for the zero casino advantage. You would of course lose your odds bet (as well as the pass line bet) should the shooter not make the point.

There are certain rules regarding the odds bet. You are permitted to make the odds bet at any time as long as you've made the pass line bet and a point is established.

You are also permitted to remove your odds bet at any time (the casinos would love for you to do this) but this should never be done.

All casinos allow players to make an odds bet equal in value to the original pass line bet (if you wager $10 on pass line, you can wager $10 odds). In addition you should make the size of your odds bet in a way that will facilitate the payoff by the dealer.

For example, the odds payoff on 5, 9 is 3 to 2. As long as you wager an even amount as odds bet when the point is 5 or 9, the dealer can easily pay off your winning odds bet by giving you 1.5 times your odds bet (that's the same as 3 to 2 payoff). If you wagered an odd amount, for example $5 in odds, the payoff in this case would be $7.50. Casinos don't like to deal in small change. Therefore they prefer and will remind players to bump up their odds bet slightly to facilitate an easy payoff. So, for example, if you wagered $5 on pass line, casinos will allow you to wager $6 in single odds when the point is 5 or 9. The $6 in odds will be paid $9 (3 to 2 payoff).

As a general rule, there is never a problem with the size of the odds bet when the point is 4 or 10. No matter what the size of the pass line bet, you just match it as single odds and the dealer can readily pay off at 2 to 1 odds.

The odds bet for points 5 and 9 should always be an even amount. You can either add one white chip ($1) to your odds bet to make it even or the casinos will allow you to add one chip in the denomination you are betting to convert an odd amount in single odds to an even amount. For example, if you had a $15 pass line bet and the point becomes 5 or 9, you are permitted to make a $20 single odds bet (4 red chips). The payoff on $20 odds bet for 5 or 9 would be $30.

In the case of the point numbers 6 or 8, you need to remember to wager $5 or multiple of $5 as single odds. The reason is that the odds payoff is $6 for every $5 wagered. Thus your odds bet should always be $5, $10, $15, $20, etc.

Here again the casinos allow some leeway to facilitate payoffs. For example, if a bettor has a $15 or $20 pass line bet, the casino would allow the player to wager $25 in single odds. The payoff for a winning $25 odds bet is a green ($25) and red ($5) chips. It's easy for the dealer to pay off $30 for a $25 wager and the player gets paid in chips he or she is probably using (red and greens).

As a beginner at craps you should find a three dollar (or less) minimum bet craps table and make the following bets. Wager $3 on pass line and then take $3 in odds on points 4 and 10, $4 in odds on 5 and 9, and $5 in odds for 6 and 8. The casino will allow the slightly increased odds bet to again help facilitate the payoffs. By betting in the above manner, the odds payoff regardless of the point is always $6.

The above can also apply to larger bets. Just remember that to get maximum single odds, bet 3 units in odds for 4 and 10, 4 units for 5 and 9, and 5 units for 6 and 8.

Don't let sizing the odds bet scare you. As a beginner, position yourself along the craps table closest to one of the two dealers responsible for payoffs. Don't be afraid to ask them for help to make the odds bet. That's part of their job and if they are helpful, a toke (or tip) would be in order (more about tipping later).

Laying Odds

Up till now, I have been discussing making an odds bet in conjunction with a pass line bet. In craps parlance, a player is taking the odds. It is also permissible to make an odds bet in conjunction with a don't pass bet, which is known as laying the odds. It is important to understand the difference between taking or laying odds.

As you already know, a player who takes the odds is betting that the point number repeats before a 7 is tossed. In this situation, because the casino has the distinct advantage (since the 7 can be rolled in more different combinations than any point number), a winning odds bet is always paid greater than even money.

Now what about the player who makes a $5 wager on the don't pass line. If 4 were thrown as the point number for example, this player may now lay the odds by placing $10 in chips on the layout next to the original bet. If a 7 is thrown before the 4 repeats, the player wins $5 (or even money) on the original $5 don't pass bet, and $5 (or 1 to 2) on the $10 odds bet.

Notice that the don't pass bettor wagers more in odds to win less. Or to put it another way, the player lays odds at less than even money. That's because once a point is established the don't pass bettor has the advantage over the casino.

The amount of odds payoff depends upon the point number. For a point of 4 or 10, you lay $10 to win $5 (1 to 2); for the 5 or 9, you lay $9 to win $6 (2 to 3); and in the case of the 6 or 8, you lay $6 to win $5 (5 to 6).

The effect of the odds bet on the don't pass is to reduce the casino's advantage from 1.4% to about 0.8%, about the same disadvantage as the pass line plus odds bettor.

As mentioned previously, chips used for the odds bet are placed not behind the line (like the pass line) but next to the original don't pass wager. The chips are usually placed bridged or heeled.

Bridging means placing, for example, one red chip next to another red chip, then placing a third red chip on top of both (or bridged). Heeling means placing, for example, one red chip next to another red chip, then placing 4 white chips on top of one of the red chips, but slightly tilted or off centered.

Odds bets are bridged if the winning odds bet payoff is the same value as the original don't pass bet. For example, if you wagered one red chip ($5) on don't pass and 10 were thrown as the point, the $10 odds bet (2 red chips) should be bridged since the $10 odds bet would win $5 (same payoff as original $5 don't pass bet). Odds bets are heeled, on the other hand, if the wining odds bet payoff is greater than the original don't pass bet. For example, if a player wagered $5 on don't pass and 9 was established as the point, the player would lay $9 in odds (to win $6) by placing one red and four white chips heeled. Don't be too frightened about whether or not to bridge or heel. As a beginner, just place your odds bet next to your original don't pass bet and the dealer will either bridge or heel the chips. After a while, you'll get the hang of when to bridge or heel.

One word of advice about removing don't pass bets from the layout. Casinos will allow it at any time and often times you'll see players do it especially if the point is 6 or 8. This is one of the craziest things to do when you play craps. Once a point has been established, the don't pass bettor has the best of it and therefore should *never* remove his or her don't pass bet.

Multiple Odds

The vast majority of casinos throughout the USA allow double odds (you can wager double in odds vs. pass line); some allow triple odds, and a few like the Horseshoe Casino in downtown Las Vegas and the President Casino in Biloxi, Mississippi offer ten times odds. As a general rule, the more you wager in odds, the lower you reduce the casino's advantage. The following table shows the relation of the pass line and odds to the casino's advantage.

	Casino's Advantage
Pass line	1.41%
Single odds	0.85%
Double odds	0.61%
Triple odds	0.47%
5 x odds	0.33%
10 x odds	0.18%

Notice that the casino's advantage can be reduced to less than 1% by making the odds bet. That's an expected casino win of less than a dollar for every $100 wagered on pass line and odds. Other than blackjack, poker and specific video poker machines played skillfully, you won't find better odds in a casino than the pass line and odds bet. (The same holds true for laying odds with a don't pass bet. See Chapter 14).

Why are the casinos advertising and promoting a bet that is actually good for the player? In reality the casinos are making a lot of money from players who make the three, five or ten times odds wager simply because these players are undercapitalized. In other words if you intend to make a $5 pass line bet then follow with a $50 odds bet, you had better have a lot more bankroll than say wagering pass line with single, double, or triple odds. Unfortunately, most craps players understand that more odds reduces the casino's edge therefore they run to casinos offering ten times odds without being properly capitalized. With $55 on the table at one time a few adverse rolls and the player is wiped out in a short period. Casinos know this which is why they still make money on such a low percentage bet for them.

The key to making the odds bet is to wager *as small as possible* on the pass line then back up the bet with multiple odds. Start with only single odds, and if you win, keep the pass line bet the same and increase your odds bet to double. Win again and increase the odds to triple. As long as you keep winning, keep increasing the odds bet up to the maximum allowed. By betting in this manner, you will be increasing the size of your bet *only when you are winning* and *only on a bet that has no casino advantage* (more about this in Chapter 13).

6

Come and
Don't Come Bets

One of the most misunderstood bets on the craps table is the come bet because the word "come" on the layout means nothing to the average player.

To define it simply, a come bet is a bet which has the same win and lose rules as the pass line bet except the come bet is made *after* the come-out roll whereas the pass line bet is made only *before* the come-out roll. Since the rules for winning are the same as the pass line bet this means that you are an immediate winner on the come bet if the next dice roll is 7 or 11; likewise you lose if it's 2, 3, or 12. If a point number is rolled, that number must repeat before a 7 is rolled to win (if a 7 is rolled first, you lose).

Let's go through a few dice rolls to explain this bet in detail. Assume you've wagered $5 on the pass line and the shooter throws a 5 on the come-out roll. Five now becomes the shooters point. You win your pass line bet, of course, if the shooter throws a 5 before a 7; you lose if the opposite occurs. But before the shooter picks up the dice, you place a $5 chip in the area of the craps layout marked

COME. On the next dice roll, you'll win this come bet if the dice total is 7 or 11. You lose this bet, if the roll is 2, 3 or 12.

Notice that a roll of 7 on this very next dice roll after you make a come bet will be a winner for your come bet but you would lose the $5 pass line bet. This is what confuses the average player, namely that the pass line bet lost and the come bet won. But keep in mind, every bet you make on the craps table is an independent bet which means one bet may win or lose independent of any other bet.

Novice players are also confused as to what happens to a come bet should the next dice roll be one of the point numbers 4, 5, 6, 8, 9 or 10. Let's say you wager a $5 come bet and the next dice roll is a six. Six has now become your come point. The dealer will pick up your $5 bet in the area marked COME and place your bet inside the six point box at the top of the layout. Thus your bet which was originally in the COME area has traveled to the six point box. You win this $5 bet if the shooter repeats your come point six before throwing a seven. You lose if a seven is rolled before the six.

Players are not limited to making only one come bet. In fact a come bet can be made before every dice roll except, as mentioned previously, before the initial come-out roll (here is where you wager on pass line). Bear in mind, each come bet can win or lose independently of the other come bets.

Making several come bets is smart play because it allows you to take advantage of a "hot roll" where point numbers are repeating without the appearance of the seven. If you have come bets on several point numbers you will be in a good position to capitalize on hot rolls (more about this in the chapter on winning strategies).

Remember that once you establish a come point number it will lose if a seven is rolled before the number. So if you have a come bet on the come points 4, 5, 6 for example and the shooter throws a 7, you lose all your bets.

To minimize this catastrophe and yet still be in a position to capitalize on the hot roll, I recommend making a maximum of *two come bets* in addition to the initial pass line bet.

The house advantage on the come bet is 1.4%. This puts this bet in the category of a "smart bet" for the player. You can lower this advantage even more by learning how to make an odds bet along with your come bet.

If you wager $5 in the COME area and the shooter throws a four, the dealer will move your $5 chip to the four point box. To make the odds bet you simply place another $5 chip in the COME area, get the dealer's attention and say loud and clear "put odds on that four." The dealer will pick up your $5 chip and place it on top of (but slightly off center) your $5 chip resting in the four point box. You now have two $5 chips "on the four." If the four is rolled before a seven, your bet wins. The bottom $5 chip will win $5. The top $5 chip (odds bet) will win, in the case of the point number four, a total of $10.

The odds bet is paid off differently for each of the come point numbers just as it is with the pass line odds bet. For the four and ten the odds payoff is 2 to 1; on the five and nine it's 3 to 2; and the six and eight odds bet pay 6 to 5. By making a single odds bet on all your come point numbers, you will reduce the house percent to a low 0.8%. Multiple odds will reduce it further just like the pass line odds bet. Other than playing blackjack skillfully, a come bet with odds is also one of the very best bets in the casino.

When you win a come bet the dealer will put your winnings in the COME area (where you initially made the bet). It's your responsibility to pick up your chips. If you don't then the chips will ride as a new come bet for the next dice roll (or in the worst scenario, another player will pick up your winnings!)

Also, once a come bet is made it cannot be removed from the layout by a player. The bet must remain on the layout until it either wins or loses. (It is a contract bet just like the pass line wager.) The odds portion of the come bet however may be removed by a player at any time (however a smart player should never do this).

In the event a player has a come bet with odds on a come-point number it is always understood that the odds are off on the come-out or first roll. If you want to have the odds bet working, you must state this to the dealer prior to the come-out by saying "keep my odds on the eight working." The dealer will acknowledge this by putting an ON button on top of your odds bet.

For example, if you had a $5 come bet with $5 odds on number 4 and on a subsequent come out roll the shooter throws a 7, normally you would only lose the initial $5 bet on 4. The $5 odds bet, since it is not a working bet on the come out roll, will be returned to you. If instead you had the odds working, you would also lose the $5 odds bet.

Likewise, in the above example if the shooter were to throw a 4 on the subsequent come out roll, your original $5 come bet on the 4 would be paid off at $5 but the $5 odds bet, since it was not working on the come out roll, would be returned to you with no payoff. If instead you had the odds working, your odds bet would receive a $10 payoff.

The reason the casino has the come odds off or not working on the come out roll is because pass line bettors are hoping for the 7 which will win their pass line bet on come out rolls. Even though a 7 wins the pass line bet, it results in a loss for all come point bets. To "lessen the blow" of losing the come point bet, the casinos have the odds portion not working.

Although logically that makes some sense, mathematically you are always better off with odds on the come bet because it reduces the casinos' edge significantly. I always, therefore, tell the dealer before each come out roll to "keep my odds working." He or she will acknowledge this by putting an *ON* button on top of one of my come odds chips. This signifies to the boxperson that the odds bets on my come numbers are working bets on the come out roll. That means they'll be paid off at true odds if the shooter throws one of my come numbers (and they will lose if the shooter throws a 7). I want the lowest possible casino edge on all my bets which is why my odds bet is always working.

Also keep in mind that if you happen to make a come bet and then on the next roll the shooter makes the point, the dealer will move your come bet to the number rolled. The next dice roll is a come out roll. Before the roll, you need to put odds on that come bet and also tell the dealer you want them "working."

Normally if one of your come point numbers hits, the dealer will pay off the original and odds bet by placing the original wager and payoff in the come betting area. In other words, the dealer moves the original chips from the come point number back to the come betting area and then pays off. If the table isn't very crowded, the dealer will often then move the chips (original and winnings) from the come betting area to right in front of the player. In either case it's your responsibility to pick up your chips.

If you make more than one come bet the dealers have a procedure called OFF and ON that they use to facilitate come point number payoffs.

Suppose you have $5 on come number 6 with $5 in odds and you make another $5 bet in the come betting area. The shooter now throws a 6 which wins your come number wager. Theoretically the dealer would move your chips from the number 6 back to the come betting area, pay off your bet with more chips, then move the new $5 come bet you just made up to the 6. You would then pick up your winning chips, put another $5 odds on the 6 and another $5 come bet. That's a lot of motion for one winning bet. To make it easier for the dealer, if he or she sees that you make more than one come bet, the dealer will use the ON and OFF technique to pay off a winning come number. In the above example, the dealer will simply pay you off $11 and on the layout he or she will leave $5 on 6 with $6 odds plus a new $5 come bet. This is quick and saves you the time of making the same bets again (in essence the dealer did it for you).

As mentioned previously, it is to your advantage to make multiple odds bets on your come numbers to reduce the casino's edge to as low as possible. The casino's edge on come bets will be reduced by making multiple odds bets, the same way it is on pass line bets. Thus double odds on a come number will reduce the casino's edge to 0.6%, triple odds to 0.5%, and so forth.

Even though you can make as many come bets as you wish after the come out roll, I would recommend that you have a maximum of two come bets on the layout. This will give you three working numbers, the point number and two come numbers. If necessary, you can also make the place bet on 6 and 8 if these numbers are not covered (more on this in the next chapter). Having 3 or 4 working numbers will allow you to capitalize on a shooter's good fortune of rolling a lot of numbers without the 7. The reason we don't want more come bets than two is because if a 7 is rolled, we lose all our bets (pass line, come bets, and all odds). This is where we are most vulnerable so a maximum of two come bets is a good balance between risk and reward.

Come betting was designed by the casino to permit continual betting on every dice roll by the right bettor. The more money bet, the greater is the casinos' profit potential since percentages are working in the casinos' favor on every bet.

By making come bets with odds you will be giving the casino little in the way of an advantage and with a little luck, you will be able to capitalize on those "hot rolls."

Don't Come

A don't come bet is the opposite of the come bet. This bet is made by the wrong bettor usually after a don't pass line bet. A don't come bet is made only on point-rolls and wins if the next roll of the dice - after the bet is made - is either a 2 or 3 and loses if instead a 7 or 11 is rolled (the 12 is a standoff). If a point number is rolled, the dealer moves the bet to the area above the number on the top of the layout and this bet wins if a 7 is rolled before this come number repeats and loses if instead this number repeats before a 7.

Players may also lay odds on don't come bets similar to laying odds on the don't pass bet. If you wager in the don't come and a point number is thrown, you lay odds by placing the chips representing the odds bet in the don't come area, getting the dealer's attention, and telling him or her to "lay odds on the 6" (or whatever come point number was rolled). The dealer positions the original don't come bet and the odds bet on the very top of the layout in the appropriate point number box. Just like laying odds on the don't pass, when you lay odds on the don't come you wager more to win less. If the come point is 4 or 10 you lay odds at 1 to 2; for the 5 or 9, you lay 2 to 3; and for the 6 and 8, you lay 5 to 6.

When the don't come bet is made with single odds the casino's advantage is reduced from 1.4 to 0.8%. Laying double odds reduces it still further to about 0.6%.

Other differences between come and don't come is the following. With the come bet, the odds are always off on the come out roll and you are not permitted to remove a come bet from the layout (the odds yes, but the original come bet, no). With the don't come bet, you are permitted to remove the bet (with odds, anytime you like). This should not however be done since once a don't come number is established, you have the edge. Don't ever remove the don't come bet!

7

Place Bets

Craps players are permitted at any time to make a bet that a particular number, either 4, 5, 6, 8, 9 or 10, will appear when the dice are tossed before a 7. The most popular way of making this kind of bet is to place the number.

First let me go through the mechanics of making a place bet. Assume for the moment you've stepped up to the craps table and you want to make a wager on the number 6. In order to make this bet, you must put your chips on the table usually in the area labeled COME, get the dealer's attention and say "place the six." The dealer will put your chips in the six numbered box at the top of the layout. In Atlantic City casinos, there is a special area within the box for place bets (you'll see the word "place" written on the layout).

The important thing to remember about making place bets is that these bets must be made by the dealer. You never put chips in the point box numbers at the top of the layout - only the dealer is permitted to place player bets in this area. In fact this is a good time to bring up who is responsible for making bets on the layout. The come betting area is sort of the dividing line between player and dealer. Any bets from come betting area toward pass line area are made by the players (that includes come, pass line, don't pass, don't come, odds, field bet, big 6 and 8 - see layout on page 4). Any bets above the come betting area are the responsibility of the dealer. You should never place chips above the come betting area - that's a NO-NO!

So you've made a place bet on the six, now what happens. Well, if the shooter throws the dice and a six appears before the seven, you win the bet. On the other hand if a seven appears before the six, you lose the bet.

For example, if the dice numbers after you made your place six bet were 3, 2, 9, 11, 6 - you'd win the bet (note that the six appeared before a seven). If instead the dice rolls were 9, 2, 12, 7 - you'd lose the bet.

When you make place bets on the numbers, you must bet in multiples of five or six dollars in order to get the maximum odds payoffs. Here's why.

The place bet on the four or ten is paid at the rate of nine dollars for every five dollars bet (9 to 5 payoff). This means your minimum wager should be $5 to win $9. If you wager less than $5, the casino will only pay off at 1 to 1 or even money - and that's not good.

The five and nine pay 7 to 5 hence the minimum bet should be $5 to win $7. It's easy to get the maximum odds payoff if you just remember to wager $5 or multiples thereof on all the numbers except 6 and 8 - the latter requires a $6 or multiples thereof wager.

Place Bet	Payoff
6, 8	7 to 6
5, 9	7 to 5
4, 10	9 to 5

Now how about your chances of winning. In order to

calculate this we must compare our true odds for winning the bet vs the casino payoff. For example, the number 4 can be rolled in only three different dice combinations (2,2; 3,1 and 1,3) whereas the 7 can be rolled six ways. Thus we have twice as many chances of rolling a 7 vs. a 4. Now when we make a place bet on the number 4, we're hoping that the shooter throws a 4 before a 7. The chances are 2 to 1 against this happening. Therefore the risk you take when you make this bet is 2 to 1 yet the casino payoff if you win is not 2 to 1 (or 10 to 5) but rather 9 to 5. Notice the casino has paid you one chip less than the risk you took when you made this bet. This one chip represents the casino's advantage and in mathematical terms, this works out to 6.66% or a loss rate of $1 per $15 wagered on this bet.

The same analysis for the other place numbers yields the following casino advantage: 4 or 10 - 6.7%; 5 or 9 - 4.0%; and 6 and 8 - 1.5%.

In order to be a winning craps player, you must minimize the casino's advantage and learn proper money management. A casino advantage of 4.0 or 6.7% for the 5, 9 or 4, 10 place bets is much too high. The 6 and 8 place bet has only a 1.5% casino advantage and is what I consider to be a borderline craps bet. I recommend making this bet only if you are experiencing a winning streak at the table, you're ahead, and the shooter is rolling a lot of numbers. Now is when you want to put money on the 6 and 8 - by placing these numbers for a minimum of $6 each (more about this in Chapter 13).

A few more items that you should know when you place the six or eight. These bets can be taken off or removed from the table any time you want to do so. Also, these bets are automatically off (or not working) on the come-out roll. When you win a place bet, the dealer will only give you your winnings ($7) and the original $6 bet will remain on the layout. If you want that back also, simply tell the dealer to "take down the six."

With a 1.5% casino advantage the 6 and 8 place bets are smart bets to make on the craps table and the intelligent right bettor will learn to use these bets to maximize profits on "hot rolls."

There is, however, a lot of confusion especially among novice players regarding the place bets. For example, a confused craps shooter once wrote to me: "Just about every book on craps states to avoid making a lot of place bets yet every time I play craps in the casino the majority of craps players are making these bets and they seem to be winning. Who's right?"

You are correct in your observation that the majority of craps players make place bets on all the numbers. But that doesn't mean it's a smart way to play craps. Here's why.

A typical craps shooter will make a bet on the pass line and then after a point is established, will throw $27 (or $26) worth of chips on the table and announce to the dealer "$27 (or $26) across." The dealer picks up the chips and spreads them almost equally on all the place numbers except the point number. For example if 4 were the point, the shooter's $27 would be placed as follows: $6 on the six, $6 on the eight, $5 on the five, $5 on the nine, and $5 on the ten. If you add up the amount bet on the place numbers, you'll see it totals $27.

Our bettor now has $27 riding on the place numbers 5, 6, 8, 9 and 10. He or she wins immediately if the shooter throws one of these numbers; however, everything is lost if instead the shooter tosses a seven. Craps shooters make place bets because they are impatient and greedy. They can't wait to win and they know by making place bets that they'll get an immediate payoff if a number hits. However, what most craps players don't know is the following.

If you make place bets on all the numbers except the point number you need at least four repeating numbers to show a profit. If this doesn't happen, you'll end up losing money. And on a cold table, four repeating numbers is tough to come by.

This plus the mathematical fact that place bets have a relatively high casino advantage simply means that the majority of place bettors will slowly but surely lose money in the long run. It's true that once in a while they'll make a big score when those place numbers start repeating but on balance, unless they happen to be extremely lucky, they will get wiped out.

And this is the reason why casinos love the high rolling place bettor, who inevitably becomes a big loser. The casinos cater to these players to keep them happy and to keep them playing.

Is there any time a craps player should make place bets? Yes there is, but it should only be limited to the six and eight because the casino's advantage is only 1.5% (compared to 6.7% for 4 and 10 and 4% on the 5 and 9). I usually make place bets on the six or eight when I'm winning and I don't have these numbers covered by a come bet. It gives me the opportunity to cover these numbers in a hot shoot.

Another craps shooter once wrote to me and asked, "I've just started to get my feet wet at the craps table but I don't understand the meaning of some of the terms I hear when players make number bets. Specifically, 'press the bet,' 'down on the number' and 'keep it working.' Can you explain?"

If a player wins a place bet, you might hear the expression "press it." The player is telling the dealer to use some of the winning place bet chips to double the bet on the place number. Whatever winning chips are left over, these are given back to the player. For example, you make a $6 place bet on the number 6. The shooter obliges and throws a six before a seven. You win the bet. The winning payoff for a $6 bet is $7. If you tell the dealer "press it" they will take $6 from the $7 you won and place it on top of the original $6 place bet on the six. The remaining $1 is given back to you. The net result of this transaction is that you now have a $12 place bet on the six and $1 in profit. You have essentially used your winnings to double your bet (this is what is meant by "press it").

Pressing up your bets in this manner is a risky venture. What happens is that even though a player is winning his place bets, by constantly "pressing it" the bulk of the player's profits are on the table rather than in his or her pocket. And one throw of a seven wipes away all the profits.

Rather than constantly pressing my winning place bets on 6 and 8, I prefer to use the following betting scheme. I wager initially $6 on 6 (or 8). If the bet wins, I take my $7 profits and wager again $6. If the bet wins again, I press to a $12 wager. One more win and I take down the bet and profits.

One of the advantages of place bets over other craps bets is the bet can be removed from the table anytime a player wants. If you have a place bet on the 6 for example and you'd like the bet returned to you, tell the dealer to "take down my place bet."

Sometimes, craps shooters would like to have their bet not in effect for one or more rolls. Rather than telling the dealer to "take down the bet" the player can announce, "off on the six." A place bet that is "OFF" means the bet is left on the number but the bet doesn't win or lose (in craps terms the bet is "not working"). A shooter can reinstate the bet by telling the dealer "I want the six working."

The place bet on 6 and 8 because of its relatively low casino advantage is a smart bet for craps players and we'll make use of it in our winning strategies (Chapter 13).

8

Buy and Lay Bets

A buy bet in craps is a bet a player can make directly on one of the point numbers - 4, 5, 6, 8, 9 or 10. In essence the player is betting that the number will repeat before the 7 appears. If this occurs the player wins the bet. If instead a 7 is rolled, the player loses the bet.

Buy bets are similar to place bets except the buy bets pay off at true odds.

Number	Place Payoff	Buy Payoff
4, 10	9 to 5	2 to 1
5, 9	7 to 5	3 to 2
6, 8	7 to 6	6 to 5

In order to get the true odds payoff on a winning buy bet, a player must pay a 5% commission at the time the buy bet is made. Since the minimum value casino chip at the craps table is $1, the casinos will charge at least a $1 commission on buy bets. Therefore, if you want to make a buy bet you should always bet at least $20, since 5 percent of $20 is $1. If you were to bet less than $20, the casino would still charge a $1 commission and their edge would be astronomical. Never do this!

To make a $20 buy bet on a number you must wager $21 in chips. The dealer will put $20 on the number and the $1 commission goes to the casino bank. The dealer will also place a buy button on top of the chips to differentiate the bet from place bets.

Buy bets can be removed by the player at any time. If you ask the dealer to "take down my buy bet" make sure he or she returns $20 plus the $1 commission. Also it is always understood that buy bets are off or not working on the come out roll unless a player requests the contrary.

If you wager a minimum $20 on the buy bets the casino edge compared to the similar place bets is as follows.

Number	Place Casino Edge	Buy Casino Edge
4, 10	6.67%	4.76%
5, 9	4.00%	4.76%
6, 8	1.52%	4.76%

As you can see, it's to the player's advantage to place the 5, 9, 6 and 8 and to buy the 4 and 10 to get the lowest casino edge.

There is a technique however, to reduce the casino's advantage on the 5 and 9 buy bets.

Most casinos do not charge a second dollar in commission on a buy bet until the player wagers $40. Thus it costs the player the same $1 to buy a number for $35 as it does for $20.

The casino's advantage for a $20 buy bet with $1 commission is 4.76 percent. A $30 buy bet with a $1 commission reduces the casino's edge to 3.23 percent. This is less than the 4.0 percent place bet on 5 and 9, therefore it pays to buy the five and nine for $30 rather than to place it.

Some casinos will allow a player to wager a $39 buy

bet and charge only $1 commission. This reduces the buy bet casino edge to a low 2.5%, the best buy percentage you can get. It's the smart way to buy the 5 and 9.

Lay Bet

A lay bet can be made on any of the point numbers and it is, in a sense, the opposite of the buy bet.

It is usually the wrong or don't place bettor that makes a lay bet. Chips are placed on the layout and the dealer is instructed to "lay bet the 8." The dealer will position the chips in the don't come box 8 and to distinguish this bet from don't come bets, would place a small disc labeled buy on top of the chips (similar to buy bets.)

The payoffs for a winning lay bet are the opposite of the buy bet namely, 1 to 2 on the 4 and 10; 2 to 3 for the 5 and 9; and 5 to 6 for the 6 and 8. These payoffs are the same as the lay odds payoff for the don't pass bet.

When a player makes a lay bet, he or she must pay a 5% commission to the casino. This commission is not based upon the amount of the wager (like the buy bet) but rather based upon the expected payoff. For example, if you lay $40 against the 4, your commission is $1 or 5% of the potential $20 winning payoff (lay bet on 4 pays 1 to 2). Thus a player who makes this wager places $41 in chips on the layout; $40 becomes the lay bet on the 4 and the casino keeps the $1 commission.

Lay bets (like buy bets) can be removed from the layout at any time. Like the buy bets, if you choose to do this, the casino will return the commission.

Lay bets are always on or working even on the come-out roll (This is different than buy bets which are always off on come-out rolls).

The casino's advantage for the lay bet is 4.0% for 6 or 8, 3.2% for 5 or 9 and 2.4% for 4 or 10. This is too high a price to pay for playing craps.

Field Bet

Beginners as well as seasoned craps players like to make a bet in the field. It's a simple bet to make; one merely has to lean over the table prior to any dice toss, place the chip(s) in the betting space labeled FIELD and with one quick toss of the dice, you've either won the bet or lost. Simple? - yes. But a smart bet - well let's find out.

The betting space on the craps layout for making the field bet is large in area compared to other craps bets. This betting space can be found on both ends of the craps table making it easy to place this bet no matter where you are standing around the table.

In the majority of casinos the following dice totals appear in bold on the layout within the field betting space: 2, 3, 4, 9, 10, 11 and 12. This means you win your field bet if any of these dice totals appear on the *next* dice roll. You lose if 5, 6, 7, or 8 is rolled. Since the bet wins or loses on one roll of the dice this bet is known appropriately as a one roll bet.

The payoffs on a winning field bet pay even money

(if you bet $5, you win $5), except the 2 and 12 pay double (here you win $10 for a $5 bet). Some casinos even pay triple on the 2 (or 12) (you win $15 for a $5 bet).

At first glance, the field bet appears to be a smart bet because there are so many numbers that could win for the player and two of them pay 2 to 1. If you add them up, you win on 7 numbers (the 2, 3, 4, 9, 10, 11 and 12) and lose on only 4 (the 5, 6, 7 and 8). To the average player this looks like a can't lose 7 to 4 proposition which is why you'll see so many players making field bets.

If we examine the simple mathematics of this bet we should be able to find out if this bet is indeed as good as it looks. What's important as far as your chances of winning and losing is not the ratio of winning to losing numbers but rather how many ways can two dice be tossed to give the winning numbers vs. the losing numbers.

The following are the different ways or dice combinations which are possible to give each of the winning field numbers.

Field Number	Dice Combinations	Ways to Make
2	1,1	1
3	1,2; 2,1	2
4	1,3; 3,1; 2,2	3
9	4,5; 5,4; 3,6; 6,3	4
10	4,6; 6,4; 5,5	3
11	5,6; 6,5	2
12	6,6	1
	Total	16

Notice that there are 16 ways or dice combinations to make the winning field bets. Let's now total the dice combinations for the numbers that will lose a field bet.

Field Number	Dice Combinations	Ways to Make
5	1,4; 4,1; 2,3; 3,2	4
6	1,5; 5,1; 2,4; 4,2; 3,3	5
7	1,6; 6,1; 2,5; 5,2; 4,3; 3,4	6
8	2,6; 6,2; 3,5; 5,3; 4,4	5
	Total	20

Although these numbers are few in number, they have more ways of being rolled (20) than the winning field numbers (16 dice totals). Thus you have a greater chance of tossing one of the losing field numbers than a winning number.

The house percent or advantage working against the player who makes field bets is 5.6% and this includes the 2 to 1 payoff on the 2 and 12. At craps tables with a 3 to 1 payoff on the 12 (or 2), the house percent is reduced to 2.8%. These percentages means the field bettor who makes a consistent $3 bet on each dice roll, will lose, on average, about $12/hr (assuming 70 dice throws per hour). At a casino with a 3 to 1 payoff on the 12, this loss rate is reduced to $6/hr.

Field bets should not be consistently made if you want to win at craps. The reason is because the house advantage is much too high and you're giving the casino too much for the privilege of making this bet. So even though the field bet gives you action on every roll and is simple to make, you will pay for this with the high house advantage.

10 Big 6 and 8

The big 6 and 8 betting area is prominently displayed at both ends of the craps layout. It is a simple bet to make and most novice craps players believe this bet has a good chance of winning because the numbers 6 and 8 are thrown very frequently.

The player who wagers on the big 6 (or 8) is betting that either the 6 (or 8) will appear on subsequent dice rolls before the 7 appears. If this occurs, the player wins. If the 7 appears instead, the bet is lost.

If this bet sounds a lot like the place bet on 6 and 8 you're correct. The difference - and it's a big one - is whereas the place bet on 6 and 8 get paid at 7 to 6, the payoff on the big 6 (or 8) is only 1 to 1.

A payoff of 1 to 1 means that a player wagering a big 6 (or 8) stands to win 5 bets on average for every 6 lost. This means an average loss rate of 1 chip for every 11 chips wagered, or a hefty casino advantage of 9.09%.

When the Atlantic City casinos first opened, the state gaming rules permitted the big 6 and 8 bet in craps but the casinos had to pay off a winning bet at 7 to 6 which was a better deal than the 1 to 1 payoff in Nevada. You still lose 6 bets for every 5 won but because of the 7 to 6 payoff, your loss rate was reduced from 1 chip for every 11 wagered to 1 chip lost for every 66 chips wagered. This dramatically cuts the casino percentage from 9.09% to only 1.5%.

So why don't the Atlantic City casinos have this bet anymore? It turns out, as more players became knowledge-able about craps and how good a bet the big 6 and 8 was, nearly everyone at the craps table was making this bet. And since this bet is made by the player, rather than the dealer, the dealers were having a tough time determining which player on the table actually made the big 6 and 8 bets. It was quite common to see five or more bets of different denomination in the big 6 and 8 betting layout. Then when the bet won, and the dealer paid off the winning bets next to each of the five or more bets on the layout, all hell broke loose as players began arguing amongst themselves whose bet was whose. This led to pandemonium at the craps tables, something the casinos would not tolerate. So they petitioned the Casino Control Commission to eliminate the bet from the layout, which the commission did.

There was actually another reason given by the casinos to eliminate this bet. There is another almost identical bet on the craps layout which the casino dealer has more control of, and that's a place bet on either the 6 or 8. To make this bet a player places his or her chips on the layout and tells the dealer to place the 6 (or 8). The dealer positions the chips in the 6 or 8 point box in a manner so that he or she knows which bet belongs to each craps player around the table. The rules for winning or losing the place 6 or 8 bet are the same as the big 6 or 8. The payoff is 7 to 6 which is a good deal for the player.

Another difference between the big 6 and 8 vs. place 6 and 8 is that the latter is not working on the come out roll but the big 6 and 8 always work.

Even though the big 6 or 8 is *not* available in

Atlantic City casinos it is in other gambling jurisdictions. And you will always see several players make this bet with its 1 to 1 payoff. Why would anyone bet the big 6 or 8 with a 9% casino advantage when the similar place bet is available elsewhere on the layout with only a 1.5% casino edge? It can only be because of the lack of knowledge of most players. You know better!

11

Proposition Bets

"Four, hard four, points four. Okay, who wants the yo-11. $5 on any craps." This is the typical jargon of the stickperson at the craps table. His or her primary job is to control the pace of the game, move the dice around the table to the shooter, and to entice players into making the high percentage proposition bets.

Basically proposition bets are the long shot bets at the craps table. They are located in the center of the layout with their payoffs clearly visible. These bets have high payoffs which is one of the reasons players make them.

There are two different types of proposition or prop bets. Most are one roll bets which means on the next roll of the dice, you either win or lose your bet. The other type of prop bet, known as the hardway bets, can stay active for more than one roll.

Casinos have two different ways to indicate on the layout what the winning payoffs are for prop bets. Some casinos list the winning payoffs on the layout with the word "to." For example, the winning payoff on the any seven prop bet is listed as 4 to 1. All Atlantic City casinos, for example,

51

must list the payoffs with "to."

Las Vegas casinos, for example, list the payoff for the same bet as 5 for 1. The difference of a 4 to 1 vs. 5 for 1 payoff is as follows.

Whenever the casino pays off a 4 to 1 bet, the player will receive $4 in winnings plus the original one dollar bet. Casinos that pay 5 for 1 will give the player $5 in winnings but keep the $1 original bet.

If you followed the above, you should realize a bet that pays 4 to 1 vs. 5 for 1 is the same. The problem that sometimes occurs is that payoffs for some prop bets may not be the same from one casino to another.

For example, the one roll bet on either 2 or 12 pays 30 to 1 in Atlantic City, 30 for 1 in Las Vegas, and 29 for 1 in some Mississippi casinos. The casino's edge translates to 13.9% in Atlantic City, 16.7% in Las Vegas, and a whopping 19.4% in Mississippi. Be wary therefore of the word "for" vs. "to" in payoffs and remember that any bet listed as 30 for 1 is the equivalent to 29 to 1.

Prop bets can be made at any time during the game. To make them, you toss your chip(s) to the stickperson and call out the bet you want to make. For example, if you want to bet $1 on any craps, you would toss a $1 chip and say loud and clear "$1 any craps." The stickperson would then repeat your bet and place the chip on the layout on any craps.

Often times, many players will be tossing chips to the stickperson calling out bets. Be certain the dealer acknowledges your bet and puts your chip(s) on the appropriate wager.

Let's review all the prop bets by starting with the hardways.

Hardway Bets

There are four hardway bets in the center of the layout. They are bets on the hardway 4, 6, 8 and 10.

When a player makes a bet on the hardway 4, for

example, the player is betting that the shooter will eventually throw the number 4 in the exact combination of 2,2. The latter is known as the hard 4. A 4 thrown as 3,1 or 1,3 is known as throwing the 4 easy. A bet on the hard 4 wins if the shooter throws the 4 hard (2,2) before throwing it easy (1,3 or 3,1) *or* before throwing a 7. If the 4 is thrown easy or the 7 appears, the hardway 4 bet is lost.

The typical payoffs on the hardway 4 and 10 is 7 to 1 and for hardway 6 and 8, 9 to 1.

Hardway bets are off, or not working, on the come-out roll. However, players can tell the dealer to keep the hardway bet working in which case the dealer will place an "on" button on top of the chip(s).

Any Seven
This is a one roll wager that wins only if a 7 is rolled immediately after the wager is made and loses if instead any other number appears. Payoff is 4 to 1.

Any Craps
This is a one roll wager that wins only if one of the craps numbers (2, 3 or 12) is rolled immediately after the wager is made and loses if instead any other number appears. Payoff is 7 to 1.

Craps 2
This is a one roll wager that wins only if the 2 (or aces) is rolled immediately after the wager is made and loses if instead any other number appears. Payoff is 30 to 1.

Craps 3
Similar to craps 2. Wins if next roll is a 3; loses on any other number. Payoff is 15 to 1.

Craps 12
Similar to craps 2. Wins if next roll is a 12; loses on any other number. Payoff is 30 to 1.

Yo-11 (Eleven)

A wager on the eleven (or "yo") wins if next dice roll is an 11; loses if any other number shows. Payoff is 15 to 1.

Horn Bet

The Horn Bet is a one roll wager that wins if any of the four numbers 2, 3, 11 or 12 is rolled immediately after the wager is made and loses if any other number appears. The Horn Bet is always made in units of $4 ($4, $8, $12, etc). If one of the winning numbers in the Horn Bet wins, you are paid at the prevailing odds payoff for that winning bet and the remaining three chips are lost to the casino. For example, if a 12 were rolled, the casino would pay you 30 to 1 but keep three chips ($3) representing losses on 2, 3 and 11.

Horn High

This is similar to Horn Bet except the player wagers in $5 multiples and designates which number, the high number, has $2 riding on it (the other numbers would have $1 riding on it). For example, a $5 Horn High 12 bet has $2 on 12, $1 on 2, $1 on 3, and $1 on 11. If one of the Horn numbers hits, the player receives the prevailing payoff for that number, the remaining chips are lost to the casino. In essence the Horn High bet is the same as the Horn Bet except one of the horn numbers has double the bet vs. the other numbers. Any of the four horn numbers - 2, 3, 11 or 12 - can be specified as the high number. Like the Horn Bet, it is a one roll bet.

Hop Bet

This is a one roll wager on any number that is not otherwise offered on the layout as a one roll wager (such as a one roll wager on number 9). The payoffs depend on whether you bet the number as a pair (such as 5,5) or non pair (such as 5,4). Betting the number 10 as a "hop bet 5,5" will pay off at 30 to 1. Betting the number 9 as a non pair (hop 5,4) pays 15 to 1. Hop bets have a high casino advantage.

Craps-Eleven

In the proposition area, there are small circles with the letters "C" and "E" inside them. This signifies a bet on craps-eleven. This is a one roll bet that craps (2, 3, 12) or 11 will be rolled on the next dice throw.

The C and E wager is actually two separate wagers. The "E" part of the wager is a bet on the yo or 11. The "C" part is the same as betting on any craps (2, 3 or 12).

One other peculiarity of prop bets that you need to be aware of is that when you win a prop bet, the dealer will only give you your winnings and the original bet is left on the layout. It's an automatic repeat wager and the stickperson will announce this on the payoff like: "Pay this gentleman $75 and you're still up to win, sir." If you don't want to bet on the next roll, you must tell the dealer "down with my prop bet."

The following table summarizes the proposition bet payoffs and casino's advantage.

Bet	Payoff	Casino's Advantage
Hard 6	9 to 1	9.1%
Hard 8	9 to 1	9.1%
Hard 4	7 to 1	11.1%
Hard 10	7 to 1	11.1%
Any seven	4 to 1	16.7%
Any craps	7 to 1	11.1%
2	30 to 1	13.9%
12	30 to 1	13.9%
3	15 to 1	11.1%
11	15 to 1	11.1%

Even though prop bets have the highest payoffs on the craps table, they are not a good bet because of the high casino edge. By anyone's recommendation, including mine, they should be avoided at all cost. Yet, if you wander past a craps table or get into a game, you'll see players constantly making these bets. Why? For one, people around the table enjoy tossing their chips to the stickperson and directing them to bet the craps, hardways, eleven, etc. Usually when a player is caught up in the excitement and feeling lucky or when he or she is trying to impress someone or simply doesn't know any better, then the prop bets are very tempting.

Still others mistakenly use the prop bet to insure their pass or don't pass line bet. For example you'll often see players insure a $15 pass line bet on the come out roll simultaneously making a $2 bet on any craps. The logic is that if the shooter throws one of the craps numbers on the come out roll, you'll lose the $15 pass line bet but win $14 (7 to 1) on the any craps bet. This reduces the player's loss to only $1 ($15 loss on pass line minus $14 won on any craps). Likewise don't pass bettors often insure their bet with a wager on the "yo" or "any seven." Don't get suckered into making these "insurance" bets. The fact of the matter is that each bet you make on the craps table is an independent bet that carries its own casino advantage. Combining one bet with another insurance bet will not alter the casino's edge. In the above examples players will lose a lot more making any craps bets simply because there is a higher probability of making all the other numbers vs. 2, 3 or 12. And when those other numbers are rolled (4, 5, 6, 7, 8, 9, 10, 11) the any craps bet is lost. Ditto for the bet on the yo and any seven.

The bottom line is that if you want insurance, go see your insurance agent. If you are serious about winning, stay away from the prop bets and stick with the bets that have the lowest casino advantage.

12

Casino Advantage

Eighteen different kinds of bets were summarized in Chapters 4 to 11. Some of those bets are very smart ones to make while others should be avoided like the plague. The deciding factor is how much of an edge does the casino have on a particular bet. This edge is called the casino advantage which means if a bet has a 5 percent casino advantage, then over a long period of time, the casino on average will keep 5% of the amount wagered on this bet. This average percent take is the casinos way of generating funds needed to pay the overhead and turn a profit.

In the game of craps, the casino's advantage varies depending upon the type of bet. And here is the golden rule to become a winning craps player:

If you are serious about winning you must limit your bets to those that have the lowest casino advantage!

The casino creates its advantage by simply not paying off a winning bet based on the true mathematical probabilities of winning that bet. Thus a player who makes a wager on any seven has a 5 to 1 chance to win yet is paid off at only 4 to 1. This difference between the casino payoff and true odds is the casino created advantage. By comparing the payoffs with true probabilities it is possible to calculate the casino advantage for all the bets. The table below lists the advantages.

BET	CASINO ADVANTAGE
Pass Line/Come	1.41%
Don't Pass/Don't Come	1.40%
Pass Line/Come with single odds	0.85%
Don't Pass/Don't Come with single odds	0.83%
Pass Line/Come with double odds	0.61%
Don't Pass/Don't Come with double odds	0.59%
Pass Line/Come with triple odds	0.47%
Don't Pass/Don't Come with triple odds	0.46%
Pass Line/Come with 5 times odds	0.33%
Don't Pass/Don't Come with 5 times odds	0.32%
Pass Line/Come with 10 times odds	0.18%
Don't Pass/Don't Come with 10 times odds	0.18%
Place 6 and 8 to win	1.52%
Place 5 and 9 to Win	4.00%
Place 4 and 10 to Win	6.67%
Buy 6 or 8	4.76%
Buy 5 or 9	4.76%
Buy 4 or 10	4.76%
Lay 6 or 8	4.00%
Lay 5 or 9	3.23%
Lay 4 or 10	2.44%
Field	5.56%
Big 6 or 8	9.09%
Any Craps	11.11%
Hardway 6 or 8	9.09%
Hardway 4 or 10	11.10%
11 or 3 proposition	11.10%
2 or 12 proposition	13.90%
Any seven	16.70%

Notice that the casino's edge varies from less than 1% to a high of 16%. This means a player who always makes a wager on any seven (16% edge) stands to lose about twenty times faster than the player who wagers on pass line with single odds (0.8%). The smart, intelligent, tough craps player is the individual who wagers only on the pass line, don't pass, the come, don't come and occasionally the place 6 or 8. In doing so he has minimized the advantage the casino has and with a good roll stands to win. Don't take my word...just watch the smiling faces of the casino floor personnel when a high rolling place and proposition bet roller saunters up to the craps table. They love him because they know the high casino advantage on these bets will "grind him down." The dealers love him because he'll probably tip like crazy. These are the players who might once in a while win but overall are losers. And they lose because they buck a high casino edge.

On the other hand, the player who limits his play to the pass line and come bets is the smart player because 1) it will be difficult and time consuming to "grind-out" such a player and 2) by having staying power at the tables the probability increases that this player will get a good roll.

13

Winning Strategies for the Right Bettor

To win at craps requires the following strategy:

1.   Be properly capitalized so that you have enough spread between your bankroll and bet size to have "staying power" at the tables.

2.   Divide your total bankroll into several session bankrolls.

3.   Never ever lose more than an allotted session bankroll at one playing session.

4.   Make bets with a low casino advantage.

5.   Increase your bets following consecutive wins.

6.   Never increase your bets following a series of loses to catch up.

7.   Set reasonable win goals and quit when they are achieved.

8.   Have patience - most of the time your session bankroll will be decreasing while you wait for the opportunity to increase your bets.

9.   Never quit on a winning streak; always on a losing streak.

The playing system I've developed and successfully used and taught to implement the above strategy is called the *Increase Odds* system. It will allow you to implement the above strategy with minimum risk to your bankroll.

One of the keys to winning at craps is to be able to capitalize on a run of numbers being rolled by steadily increasing your bets. And the best place to increase your bet is on a bet that has no advantage to the casino - the odds bet!

The Increase Odds system works as follows:

1.   Make an initial bet on pass line with the lowest bet possible (e.g. $5 at $5 minimum table).

2.   After a point is established, make a single odds wager, and then make a $5 come bet. Put single odds on your come after it travels to the come point number. Make a second come bet with single odds; then stop betting.

3.   The goal is to have two come bets working with single odds along with pass line and odds. Do *not* have more than two come bets.

4.   When either the pass line point or one of the come numbers wins, maintain a $5 bet size but then increase all subsequent odds bets to $10 (double odds).

5.   If your bets continue to win then continue to increase your odds on pass line and come as follows: 2x, 3x, 4x, 5x, 6x, etc. For the more conservative player, wait for two consecutive wins at one level before you increase to the next level (2x, 2x, 3x, 3x, 4x, 4x, etc.).

6.   Any time you lose one of your bets (either pass line or come), immediately reduce your odds bet to $5 (single odds).

7.   When a player sevens out and the dice pass to a new shooter, do *not* place a wager until the shooter wins a bet (either by throwing a natural on come out or making the point). In essence, you will be waiting for an eligible shooter to start betting.

8.   If you are ahead for the session, if you've won three consecutive bets, and if you don't have either the 6 or 8 covered by come bets or as the pass line point, then make a $6 place bet on the 6 and 8. Your goal is to win three place bets on 6 (or 8) and then take down these bets. Wager on 6 and/or 8 as follows: $6 win, $6 win, $12 win, then take down.

Let's analyze the above playing method. First, you'll be making bets with less than 1% casino advantage. You'll also be increasing your bets following consecutive wins to take advantage of a hot roll. More importantly you'll be putting more money on the table with a bet (odds) that has no casino edge. You'll have at least three numbers working, enough to capitalize on a hot shoot and after you've built up profits from three consecutive wins, you'll cover the 6 and 8 with a bet with only a 1.5% casino edge. You'll never increase your bets when losing. And by waiting for the shooter to achieve one winning bet, you'll have patience. If the dice are cold and passing around the table because no one can make their point, you'll have lost nothing. Patience pays off!

I trust you agree this is a sound method to play craps. It fits all the requirements of the strategy you need to be a winner.

Money Management

To implement the Increase Odds system, you should have a total bankroll equal to 10 times the minimum basic betting unit.

Minimum Bet	Bankroll
$3	$300
$5	$500
$10	$1000
$25	$2500

It's important to be properly capitalized to withstand the sometimes wild fluctuations in a player's bankroll that occur at the craps table. Furthermore, you must adhere to the following rule:

Always divide your bankroll into at least 3 playing session bankrolls. Each of these playing sessions are independent of the other. You never lose more than the allocated bankroll at any one session.

For example, if you have a $500 bankroll, divide it into three $170 (approximately) session bankrolls and make your basic bet on pass line and come at $5.

Your win goal for each playing session is to win a minimum of 50% of your playing session bankroll. For a $170 session bankroll this is a win goal of $80 (rounded). If you manage to win $80, continue to play and set a new win goal of $160. As long as you continue to win, keep increasing your win goals by $80. Now here is the key to quitting.

As soon as your profits drop below the last established win goal, take the money (profits) and run!

You will never, ever, ever be a winner at craps if you don't adhere to this rule. Once you've racked up profits, it's an absolute cardinal sin to lose those profits back to the casino. This is what you see the majority of craps players do day in and day out. They are guaranteed losers because:

1. They make bets with a high casino edge.

2. They press when they lose.

3. They are the greediest players on earth - no matter how much they get ahead, it's never enough.

What will the above win goal accomplish for you? First, it will <u>never</u> limit the amount of money you can win at one playing session. I and my students have won a bundle on sessions where nothing but numbers are being rolled and we increase our odds bets and win goals. Secondly, we are not greedy and set reasonable expectations of winning 50% of our starting session bankroll. Third, we never limit the amount we can win by increasing our win goals once the last one was achieved. And fourth and most importantly, by quitting when our luck turns and our profits drop below the last win goal achieved, we discipline ourselves to take our profits and run!

You need to keep track of how much bankroll (chips) you have during the course of play so you know where you stand toward achieving your win goal.

The easiest way to do this is to put the initial $170 in chips in the front rails and as you win, put your winning chips in a separate (behind) rail. When you manage to get ahead, leave the $170 in chips untouched and make your wagers with chips from the "profit" rail. Once you exceed the $80 win goal, set those chips aside or use a different colored chip (white chip for example) to mark the row of ($80) chips profit. Keep betting with the leftover chips (profits) and keep marking your $80 profit rows. Once you lose a bet or bets and your "profit row" of chips decreases below last win goal achieved, it's time to "color up" and walk.

Here are additional tips to help you implement the Increase Odds system.

1.   A playing session doesn't necessarily have to start and end at the same table. If my starting bankroll steadily goes south because no one at the table can seem to put together a string of numbers, I generally will leave the table after I've lost about a third of my bankroll (ca. $60). At the worst this gives you a cycle of two pass line/odds plus two come bets/odds to make something happen. If you lose your first pass line and two come bets with odds without one number winning, you'll lose $30. If it happens again, you'll be out $60. Now's the time to take a break and try another table with the leftover $110 session bankroll.

2.   Your whole strategy is dependent upon someone throwing a lot of repeat numbers. If this doesn't happen, don't expect to win. What you'll have by betting the minimum and waiting for the eligible shooter is staying power at the tables. This is all you can hope for - to be around when and if a hot shoot occurs.

3.   The strategy for waiting for an eligible shooter is to hopefully be able to bet on someone that is on the start of a hot shoot. There is absolutely nothing scientific about waiting but this technique helps me to be patient at the craps tables. Surely, there will come the time when you patiently wait for a new shooter to make his/her point so that you can bet on him/her, and the shooter throws nothing but numbers. And there you stand, watching everyone make money while you have no bets on the table. This has happened to me on several occasions. But this will be equally offset by the times the dice pass around the table

without anyone making a point and you're the only player not betting while everyone else goes down the tubes. Stick with the system and be patient. Don't bet until you have an eligible shooter!

4. Once I win my pass line or one of the come bets, I increase my odds bet on *all* subsequent bets. Thus if I win the pass line, I increase the odds on the next pass line bet and subsequent come bets. Essentially *all* the odds go up following a win and likewise they all go down to single odds following a loss.

5. If a shooter throws a natural on come out I just set aside the winning chip as profit. I keep the pass line bet the same. Ditto for a natural on the initial come bet. Likewise if I lose to a craps, I just replace the bet with the same bet size.

6. If you can't afford the $500 bankroll to bet a minimum of $5 then you have two choices. Either go find a $2 or $3 minimum bet table or start your betting at $5 pass line without odds. When the latter wins then progress to single odds, then double, etc. For the absolute beginner who wants to test the waters first, I suggest limiting your betting to pass line with single odds (don't make any come bets). If you win, then increase your odds bet on pass line.

7. For the $25 and up player who wants to get every possible edge, I would suggest you start your betting at $25 pass line with $50 double odds. Then you increase your odds to triple, and so forth as you win.

8. If you are playing at a casino that only allows a maximum of double or triple odds, you need to modify your strategy. After you've reached the maximum odds allowed and you win, you should then increase your subsequent pass line and come bets by ca. 50% and maintain your maximum odds.

The following tables show examples of how the bets are increased, following consecutive wins.

$5 Bettor / Maximum Double Odds

Base Bet	Odds	At risk	Potential Win*
$5	$5	$10	$11 to $15
$5	$10	$15	$17 to $25
$8	$16(or 15)	$24 (23)	$26 to $40
$10	$20	$30	$34 to $50

$10 Bettor / Maximum Triple Odds

Base Bet	Odds	At risk	Potential Win*
$10	$10	$20	$22 to $30
$10	$20	$30	$34 to $50
$10	$30	$40	$46 to $70
$15	$45 (50)	$60 (65)	$75 to $105
$20	$60	$80	$92 to $140

*depends on point number

The point is to first use the odds bet to increase your bets following consecutive wins and then when you reach the maximum odds allowed, start increasing your base bet by about 50% maintaining the maximum odds allowed. This technique will allow you to continue to increase your bets on a hot roll while maintaining some profits on each winning roll. Above all, when a loss occurs revert back to the base bet and single odds!

9.   Never switch your bets from pass line to don't pass or be tempted to throw a chip on C/E or other high payoff bets. You came to the table with a strategy and it's important you stick with it. Nothing can be more devastating

to a craps player than to be betting on pass line and losing then switching to don't pass and watching in disbelief as the shooter throws nothing but number after number. Stick with the strategy - if you are steadily losing, switch tables not strategy.

10. If you're planning a weekend (or week) trip to a gambling resort, you need to modify your bankroll and session banks. You need to decide beforehand how much you will take to gamble (bankroll) then divide that bankroll by number of gambling sessions. I would never play more than two sessions per day - that's plenty of gambling over an extended weekend. And never lose more than the allocated session bankroll!

Suppose you're going to Vegas for a 4 day trip and you've set aside $1000 to gamble at craps. Figure on 8 sessions (2 per day). Each session bankroll should be $125. With that size session bankroll, I would suggest a base bet of $5 (or less).

Whether you are a beginner, average player, or high roller, the above strategy will work for you, but only if you:

1. Have an adequate bankroll and never lose more than the allocated session bankroll.

2. Set your session win goal.

3. Wait for the eligible shooter before betting.

4. Use the odds bet to increase your bets following consecutive wins.

5. Limit your bets to pass line and two come bets.

6. Never increase your bets following a loss.

This is a winning strategy for you!!

14

Winning Strategies for the Wrong Bettor

There is nothing wrong with betting wrong. Even though you will be in the minority at the craps table, you can still win a bundle if you bet wrong and the table is ice cold (that's the expression for a craps table where no one can make a point and the dice keep passing from one player to the next).

Your strategy as a wrong bettor is similar to the pass line bettor except you'll be laying odds instead of taking them.

There is always a lot of controversy about laying double, triple, or more odds. Some authors and players mistakenly believe that laying odds on the don't side dilutes the edge a player enjoys once a point is established. Although they are correct in saying the don't player has the edge once a point is established, it's incorrect to say the player's edge is diluted by making an odds bet where the player (or casino) have no advantage. The fact of the matter is that even though a player must put out more money when he lays odds, he will be paid true odds if the bet wins.

71

That's all that matters. And when you get a true odds payoff, the combined don't pass and odds bet have a casino edge that is lower than just a don't pass bet.

Bet	Casino's Advantage
Don't pass	1.40%
Don't pass with single odds	0.83%
Don't pass with double odds	0.59%
Don't pass with triple odds	0.46%
Don't pass with 5 x odds	0.32%
Don't pass with 10 x odds	0.18%

To use the increase odds system on the don't pass, just do the following:

1.   Make your basic wager on don't pass with single odds and make a maximum of two don't come bets with single odds.

2.   When the bet wins, keep the size of don't pass the same and increase the odds to double.

3.   Use the same strategy to escalate the odds up to the maximum allowed. Then increase your base bet by 50% with maximum odds as discussed in pass line rules.

All the other rules should follow the strategies discussed for pass line including the determinations of bankroll, session bankroll, and win goals.

If you decide to bet the don't pass, it's best to position yourself close to the dealer so you can reach the don't come betting area. Also, please don't root out loud for the 7 - otherwise you will be upsetting a whole bunch of right bettors. Remember when you win, they are all losing!

Here is an example of implementing the increase odds system on the don't side. It assumes the player is a $10 basic bettor and the casino allows up to a maximum of triple odds.

Total bankroll:	$1000
Session Bankroll:	ca $330 for each session (3 sessions)
Base Bet on Don't Pass and Don't Come:	$10 with $20 single odds
Win Goal:	$160

You would increase your bet following consecutive wins as follows:

Base Bet	Odds	Total at Risk
$10	$20	$30
$10	$40	$50
$10	$60	$70
$15	$90	$105
$20	$120	$140

As you can see by the above example, the don't bettor will have more money at risk compared to the pass line bettor since the don't player must lay odds when he has the edge. To prevent from getting totally wiped out by a shooter that starts rolling numbers like crazy, you must always do the following:

Once a shooter throws a repeat number that makes you lose either your don't pass or don't come bet, *stop* betting on this shooter.

In essence you will not make any other bets until this shooter finally sevens out and the dice pass to a new shooter. This new shooter becomes an eligible shooter for you to bet on.

With the above strategy you'll lose a maximum of three bets with odds should a shooter go crazy with numbers. Sometimes, but not too often, this will happen so be prepared. If you were to continually replace your losing don't pass and don't come bets to a hot shooter, it wouldn't be too long before you would be totally wiped out. Don't let this happen!!

If you lose to a natural or win on a 2 or 3 on a come out roll, just maintain the same size bet on the next wager. Also maintain the same win goals (50% of session bankroll) as pass line strategy. For more conservative players, wait until you win twice at the same level of odds *before* increasing your odds bet to the next level.

I'm often asked "is it better to bet right or wrong?" Perhaps the following story will clarify this point.

Betting Right or Wrong

Wherever craps shooters meet, the question of the advantages and disadvantages of betting right or wrong usually becomes the topic of conversation. Let's see if we can logically determine which is the better bet.

Assume Fred puts up $10 on the pass line and his buddy Sam puts $10 on don't pass. What are Fred and Sam's chances of winning on the come-out roll?

We know that on the come-out roll, a 7 and 11 will make Fred a big winner. And there are 6 different ways of aligning the two die to give a 7, namely 6,1; 1,6; 2,5; 5,2; 4,3; and 3,4. There are 2 ways to throw the 11, namely 6,5 and 5,6. Thus Fred has a total of 8 combinations that could win for him. Sam, on the other hand, can only win on the come-out roll if a 2 or 3 is rolled. The number of combinations that will give a 2 or 3 are 3 (1,1; 1,2; 2,1). So on the come-out roll, Fred who is betting right on the pass line has an 8 to 3 advantage of winning vs. Sam who is betting wrong or on the don't pass line.

This is a universal fact. On the come-out roll in craps the right bettor has a much better chance of winning than the wrong bettor.

This advantage, however, changes if the shooter on the come-out roll throws a point number (4, 5, 6, 8, 9 or 10). If a point is established, Fred wins his pass line bet only if the shooter throws the point number again before a 7 is thrown. Since we know that 7 is the most prevalent number that appears when two dice are thrown, Fred now is at a disadvantage. A 7 will make him lose. He instead wants the point number thrown. His disadvantage varies depending upon the point number. If the point is 4 or 10, he faces a 2 to 1 disadvantage; if the point is 5 or 9, his disadvantage is 3 to 2, and on the 6 and 8 it is 6 to 5.

Now how about Sam, our wrong bettor. Remember that his chances of winning on the come-out roll were not very good. But if a point number is established, he wins if a 7 is thrown before the point repeats. And as we know 7 is the most prevalent number, therefore once a point has been established, Sam betting wrong is favored to win over Fred, betting right.

Once again here's the difference of betting right vs. wrong. On the come-out, the right bettor has the advantage. Once a point is established, the advantage switches to the wrong bettor.

The question now to ask is how much of the time will the right bettor have the advantage vs. the wrong bettor. Based upon a mathematical analysis of the game of craps, about one third of the time a decision will be effected on the come-out roll (i.e. someone will throw a 7, 11, 2 or 3). The remaining two thirds of the time, there will be a win or lose decision on a point roll. This means that one-third of the time right bettors on the craps table will have the advantage whereas the wrong bettor will have the advantage two thirds of the time. Psychologically it is nice to know that you have the advantage two thirds of the time which is one reason why many craps shooters bet on the wrong side or don't pass line.

Consider also the fact that most right bettors make

more than just a pass line bet. The recommended number of bets is a pass line with two come bets, all with odds. Likewise, the wrong bettor should have a don't pass bet with two don't come bets all with odds.

In the situation just described, the right bettor, as you know, stands to lose all his bets on just one roll of the dice (if a 7 is rolled, all of his bets are lost). On the other hand, in order for the wrong bettor to lose all his bets, each of the numbers must repeat. One roll of the dice doesn't wipe him out. In fact, with one roll of the dice, the wrong bettor stands to win all his bets (if a 7 is rolled).

I like to bet wrong for the reasons cited above. I like to know I have the advantage two thirds of the time and I also like to know that one roll of the dice won't wipe me out. If the table is choppy meaning there is no long string of numbers in between the 7's, the wrong bettor stands to win a lot of money. If a hot roll occurs, and a shooter throws lots of numbers, the wrong bettor can get wiped out in a hurry. To minimize this from occurring, I use a trick that the late craps expert, Sam Grafstein taught me. When I bet wrong, I'll make my don't pass and don't come bets all with odds but as soon as one bet loses I stop betting on this shooter. In this way I'll cut my losses should the shooter get his hot roll.

Keep in mind that, statistically, the casino has the same mathematical long term advantage over both the right vs. wrong bettor. But betting wrong does have its short term advantages and for this reason, should be considered when you play craps.

15

Removing Bets
from the Layout

This chapter summarizes which bets on the craps layout can be removed or taken off by the player anytime he or she wants and which bets cannot.

As I mentioned earlier, it's important you understand the above because some players who take down or remove their craps bets are actually giving away their advantage to the casino. You might find this hard to believe but I see this very thing happen on most of my casino trips.

A player makes a $10 bet on the don't pass and the shooter throws an 8 as the point number. This player immediately takes his bet off the layout, which any intelligent player should never do because once the point of 8 is established, the don't bettor has the advantage over the casino.

In the case of the don't pass bet, the casino will gladly allow you to remove your bet once a point is established. It is not because the casinos are doing us a favor, but rather because they would be happy to have a bet removed from the layout in which the casinos don't have the advantage. And by allowing uninformed players to remove this bet, the casinos over the long run are saving money.

Pass Line bet - you definitely are not permitted to remove this bet from the layout until it either wins or loses.

Don't Pass bet - can be removed by a player at any time. However, removing the don't pass bet from the layout is one of the most ridiculous plays any gambler could ever make. Don't do it!

Any Craps bet - can be removed from the layout anytime. Please note that when this bet is won, the dealer will only give the player the winnings and the original chip bet on any craps stays up for the next roll. If you want the original bet returned to you, you must tell the dealer to "take down the any craps bet." This rule holds for all proposition bets.

The Hardways - can be removed anytime.

7, 11, 2, 3, 12 - these are all one roll bets. When they win you can ask the dealer to "take down the bet."

Place bet - can be removed anytime. Also, place bets are always automatically off (or not working) on all come out rolls.

Buy bet - can be removed anytime. If you do decide to remove a buy bet from the layout, be sure the dealer returns your 5% commission.

Lay bet - can be removed anytime. Again make sure the 5% commission is returned to you.

Field bet - this is a one roll bet.

Come bet - once a come point number is established, you are not permitted to remove the bet from the layout.

Don't Come bet - you may remove this bet from the layout once a come point number is established. However, as in the case of the don't pass line bet, this should never be done since you will be giving up your advantage to the casino.

Odds bet - a player may remove the odds bet on any pass line, don't pass, come or don't come bet.

And finally, here's a suggestion to make a lot of money at the craps table. If you ever see an uninformed gambler removing his don't pass bet from the layout after a point is established, ask him if you can buy the bet from him. If he has $10 on don't pass, give him $10 and take over his bet. You'll have a 100% guarantee of showing a profit over the long run by doing this.

16
Hedge Betting

This method of betting is for the ultra conservative player. It offers an alternative betting strategy to the Increase Odds system. It works like this.

You start the betting by making a $3 bet on the don't pass line. Of course if the shooter throws a 2 or 3 on the come-out roll you win $3; if instead a 7 or 11 is rolled you lose your $3. If a point is established you now lay $6 in odds. Your next bet in the Hedge method is $3 on the come. If a 4 or 11 is rolled take $3 in odds; if 5 or 9, take $4 in odds, and if 6 or 8 take $5 in odds. Make one more come bet with odds and that is it.

What is so special about this method of betting. Well, let's compare it to betting the pass line and come with odds. A player who bets in this manner is considered tough to beat by the casino personnel. With a little luck and a few hot rolls, this player can make a nice profit. And in the long run he won't get hurt too much because his pass line and come bets with odds have a house percentage of less than 1%.

Still, a player who bets in this manner is vulnerable if a shooter throws the 7 after his bets are made. After all, a 7 is a loser for the pass line and all come bets.

This Hedge method is a way of keeping the 7 under control so we won't get wiped out on one roll. Why? Because our don't pass bet will be a winner every time a shooter sevens out.

In fact, the best thing that could happen to us is we make our don't pass bet, lay odds, then make our come bet and the shooter now throws a 7. If this occurs, we win all our bets.

This system of betting on the craps table will succeed when the dice are running cold, *i.e.* no one can hold the dice for more than one or two rolls or even if the dice turn hot and numbers are being rolled like crazy.

There is a catch. Call it the price you must pay to bet in a conservative manner via the Hedge system. If a shooter gets a real hot streak going, a Hedge bettor will not make as much profit as the player betting strictly pass line and come. However, the Hedge bettor will lose less in the case of a very cold table. In short, the Hedge method will cut down on your losses but you'll also win less on hot rolls.

There is one more twist to the system that I use to try to capitalize on a real hot streak. If I bet don't pass, lay odds and make my two come bets with odds and I find a shooter throwing nothing but number after number, I will place the 6 and 8 if they aren't covered with come bets. If the shooter makes his point (in which case I lose my don't pass bet), I switch and bet on the pass line with odds. I'm now in the position to take advantage of a possible hot roll. (This is the only time I ever switch from don't pass to pass line).

There are other hedge type betting systems being touted by so called knowledgeable players which I do not recommend. These include:

1. Make a large bet on pass line and "insuring"

yourself against the shooter throwing a craps number on the come out roll by making a dollar bet on any craps.

2.   Bet the don't pass and then make a bet on the yo'leven or any seven on the come out roll.

3.   Bet the pass line and field.

The problem with these hedge type betting systems is that you usually combine a good low percentage bet with one that has a high casino advantage. Remember that each bet you make in craps has its own independent loss rate (governed by the casino's advantage) and combining one bet with another will not alter this fact.

17

Multiple Odds Revisited

Percentage wise, double odds reduces the casino advantage to only 0.6% which is why most experts recommend to "always take double odds". But do the percentages really tell the whole story? Let's see.

Assume that Sam and Al go to the same craps table and bet in the following manner.

Al makes 100 - $10 bets on pass line; Sam makes 100 - $10 bets on pass line with double odds. Which of these betting methods would you expect to minimize the expected rate of dollar loss?

This is easy to figure out. If Al makes 100 bets of $10, he will put $1000 (100 x $10) of his money into action on the craps table. Mathematically we know that the casino's expected take or advantage for pass line bets is 1.4%. Therefore multiplying the $1000 put into action times the 1.4% yields an expected loss of $14. To put it simply, Al could lose more than this or win, but over the long term his expected loss rate is $14. Now let's calculate the expected loss for Sam who is making $10 bets on pass line but backing it up with double odds. Surely the double odds reduces the casino's advantage and we would expect a lower expected loss for Sam's style of betting (pass line with double odds) vs. Al's (only pass line).

Sam makes 100 - $10 bets on pass line so he puts $1000 of his money into action. But every time a point number is established, which should statistically occur about two thirds of the come out rolls, Sam will also be making his double odds bet. Therefore two thirds of the 100 bets Sam makes, he will be putting out besides his $10 pass line bet, another $20 bet as double odds. The total amount of money he will have in action is $1000 plus two thirds of $2000 (money used for double odds) or total of $2333. Even if you can't follow the math, the important point to remember is that Sam will be risking a lot more money by making the double odds bet ($2333) than Al who only makes the pass line bet ($1000). We know that the casino's advantage for pass line and double odds is 0.6%. Therefore Sam risks $2333 of which the casino expects to keep 0.6% of this or, you guessed it, $14. This is the same expected loss rate as Al who didn't make the odds bet.

So what does this all mean? Simply put, by making the double odds bet all you are accomplishing is putting more money into action. In effect this reduces the casinos advantage percentage-wise but because the total amount risked increased, the expected dollar loss remains the same.

But, you say, there must be some advantage to taking double odds, after all it's part of our Increased Odds betting system discussed in Chapter 13. There is. For the same fixed bankroll you are always better off making a $10 pass line bet with $20 double odds rather than making only a $30 pass line bet. In other words, don't make one large bet on the pass line but rather split the bet up into two smaller bets getting as much as you can as the back-up or odds bet. Doing this will significantly decrease your expected loss rate simply because with a fixed bankroll, you can't put more money into action.

The key point to remember is that even though double odds lowers the casino percentage for the pass line and odds bet, it also makes players risk more money in the process. If things go well when you bet double odds (or higher), you can win a bundle quickly. But if it doesn't go well, with double odds you can get wiped out just as quickly. To minimize this risk of multiple odds betting, use the technique discussed in the Increased Odds system (Chapter 13). Only bet double odds (or higher) after you win a bet with single odds.

The important points to remember are:

1.   You are always better off by betting $5 on pass line with $5 in odds than betting the entire $10 only on pass line.

2.   Bet as small as practical on pass line and bet more when you are winning on odds bet.

Learn and use these principles when you play craps and you will be significantly increasing your chances of walking away from the tables with profits.

18

Never Ever Craps

"Never Ever Craps. You never lose on the come out roll." So states the advertisement from one of the Mississippi casinos that recently introduced this new craps game. Not losing on the come out roll sounds like a good deal. Or is it? Let's take a closer look at all the rules, then decide.

In the standard craps casino game, players who wager on the pass line win their bet on the come out roll if the shooter throws a 7 or 11. If instead a 2, 3, or 12 is rolled these numbers are known as the craps numbers and you would lose your pass line bet.

In Never Ever Craps, you can't lose on 2, 3, or 12 on the come out roll. If a shooter throws one of these numbers it becomes the shooter's point, just like the 4, 5, 6, 8, 9, 10 in the standard game. Also, the natural 11 does not win on the come out roll like the standard game. It also will become a shooter's point. Therefore when you make a pass line bet in Never Ever Craps, if a 7 is rolled you win. If any other number is thrown, it becomes the shooter's point.

In the standard game once a point is established a

pass line bettor can make an odds bet on the point number. You can also do the same on the point numbers 2, 3, 11 and 12 in this new game. The casino payoff on a winning odds bet for these numbers is 6 to 1 on the 2 and 12 and 3 to 1 on 3 and 11.

The craps layout also looks different. The don't pass line bet is not available in Never Ever Craps, and the area at the top of the layout that contains the point numbers now includes the 2, 3, 11, 12 besides the standard 4, 5, 6, 8, 9 and 10.

Most craps players have ugly memories of the times they've lost a big bet on the pass line to a shooter who threw a craps number. Sooner or later it happens to all craps players. Therefore eliminating these numbers as losing bets on the come out roll sure sounds like a good deal. But you don't get something for nothing. And the price you pay for not losing on the come out roll is first, you don't win if an 11 is thrown, and second the odds of winning your pass line bet when 2, 3, 11 or 12 becomes the point are not very good.

Sitting down with my pencil, pad, a calculator and the rules of this new game, I was able to compute the casino's edge for the pass line bettor. It calculates to 5.3% which is about four times higher than the casino's edge in the standard game. Taking single, double or triple odds will reduce the edge to 2.9, 2.0 and 1.5% respectively. But this is still higher than the corresponding edge in the standard game.

In Never Ever Craps you are permitted to make place bets on the point numbers including the 2, 3, 11 and 12. The casino payoff is 11 to 2 on 2 and 12, and 11 to 4 on 3 and 11. This calculates to a casino edge of 7.1% (2 and 12) and 6.2% (3 and 11). These are not very good craps bets compared to other bets available in the standard game.

Actually this modified version of the standard craps game where you can't lose on the come out roll was first introduced in Las Vegas in the early 1980's by Bob Stupak.

Many of you have probably read Stupak's ads for his virtually free Las Vegas vacations at his casino on the strip. Bob was a maverick in the industry introducing new games like crapless craps (aka Never Ever Craps) and double exposure blackjack where both dealer cards are shown to the player.

Although this new version of craps is getting a lot of play, it remains to be seen what will happen when the novelty wears off. Although it may be fun to play craps where you never lose on the come out roll, I still prefer to play at the standard game where I can make bets with a lower casino edge.

19

Live Video Craps

It's now possible to play craps in a casino without any dealers with the new live video craps game that has been introduced in several casinos.

The game is played on a rectangular table which contains a video screen that simulates the craps layout. The layout is different than the normal craps layout since you can't make don't pass and don't come bets. Bets allowed include pass line, come, field bets, place bets on all the numbers from 2 through 12 (except 7), hardway bets on 4, 6, 8, 10 and the proposition bets which are one roll bets on any 7, any craps, the bets on the 2, 3, 11 and 12. Only single odds are allowed on pass line and come bets.

In this game, pass line bettors win if 7 is rolled on the come out roll. Any other number rolled becomes the shooter's point (including 2, 3, 12 and 11). Players use a trackball to place an arrow on the layout where they want to wager and then push a button to indicate the size of the bet. The computer will wait about 30 seconds to allow players to make their bets, then announce for one player to

93

roll the dice by spinning the trackball. When the latter is done a pair of simulated dice will fly across the table, bounce off the sides with sound effects and then come to rest. The computer will announce the number rolled then automatically pay off the winning bets, collect losing bets (with a simulated rake that sweeps the losing bets from the table!), then announce to the players to make their bets prior to the next roll.

Players can insert up to 99 units in credits prior to making bets. As the players make bets, the amount of the bet is deducted from their credit. When they win a bet, it's added to their credit. A credit meter at each player's station keeps track of each player's bankroll. At any time a player can cash out.

You must bet the pass line if you want to roll the dice. Even though the computer allows a certain time for players to make their bets, you need to be fairly quick in positioning your bets with the trackball because the computer gives no advanced notice of "no more bets."

The payoffs listed on the table for the various hardways and proposition bets are listed as "for" rather than "to." What this means is that on the standard table the payoff for a winning hardway 6 bet is listed as 9 to 1 or 9-1. Your initial one chip wins you nine more chips. On the electronic version, the payoff for the same bet is listed as 10 for 1. This means you win 10 chips but the computer keeps the initial one chip wager. Your net win is still 9 chips. In other words, 9 to 1 is the same as 10 for 1.

The payoffs and corresponding casino advantage for all bets is summarized on page 96. For the majority of the bets, the casino's advantage is the same as the standard table. Notable exceptions are the place 6/8, prop bets on 2/12 and 3/11, and pass line.

The advantage of live video craps vs the standard table game is the lower minimum bet requirements. For example, in a Mississippi casino that offers this game, they have one machine set for a $1 minimum bet and the other at 25 cents. With these low minimums, this game offers the low stakes player an opportunity to learn and play craps at low risk. Also, beginners can sometimes be intimidated by other craps players at the standard game. Live video craps eliminates this fear. However, because of the differences in the come out rules for the pass line, the casino's advantage is higher for pass line (5.3%) than the standard game (1.4%). Making the maximum single odds bet will lower it to 2.9%.

You also need to be aware that these machines only pay out in even dollar amounts. Thus if you make a bet with fractional odds such as 2.3, 3.5, etc., the machine will round down to an even dollar amount. Therefore, if you want to play live video craps you should place bets in amounts that will round to an even dollar payoff. The data below summarizes what should be your bet size to get the full odds payoff.

	Bet Size	**Payoff**
Place 2/12	2 units	13 units
Place 3/11	2 units	7 units
Place 4/10	5 units	14 units
Place 5/9	5 units	12 units
Place 6/8	7 units	15 units
Odds 5/9	2 units	5 units
Odds 6/8	5 units	11 units

Live Video Craps
Casino's Advantage

Bet	Payoff	Casino's Advantage
Pass line	2 for 1	5.3%
Pass line with single odds	see below	2.9%
Place 2 and 12	6.5 for 1	7.1%
Place 3 and 11	3.5 for 1	12.5%
Place 4 and 10	2.8 for 1	6.7%
Place 5 and 9	2.4 for 1	4.0%
Place 6 and 8	2.15 for 1	2.3%
Hardway 4 and 10	8 for 1	11.1%
Hardway 6 and 8	10 for 1	9.1%
Any seven	5 for 1	16.7%
Any craps	8 for 1	11.1%
Prop 2 and 12	30 for 1	16.7%
Prop 3 and 11	15 for 1	16.7%

Odds Bet	Payoff
2 and 12	7 for 1
3 and 11	4 for 1
4 and 10	3 for 1
5 and 9	2.5 for 1
6 and 8	2.2 for 1

20

Systems

Craps playing systems are nothing more than a predetermined plan that includes where to bet and how much to bet. Often the betting size is dependent upon whether the previous bet won or lost.

On the positive side, craps systems take the subjectivity out of the game. The system tells you "what to do" at all times and as long as you are not wagering on the high percentage craps bets, there is nothing wrong with following a systematic method of playing and betting.

On the negative side, many "system sellers" would have you believe that their system will turn the odds in your favor. This is not so. If you remember anything from this book, remember this - no betting system will reduce or eliminate the casino's edge in craps.

Having said all this, I will proceed to describe several different types of craps systems which I have used over the years. The best system still remains the Increase Odds system, but to add some variety and fun to your future craps playing sessions, you may want to consider these.

Beginners Don't Pass

I have taught this easy beginners craps playing and betting system to many individuals that have never played craps before. It's a great starter system that can be used until confidence is achieved and the player can then advance to the Increase Odds system.

The key to this system is *discipline*. You don't bet on every shooter which means some of the time you'll just be standing watching the action rather than playing. But your patience will be rewarded. Here it is:

1.   You bet only on the don't pass.

2.   As soon as a player makes his/her point or rolls a natural on the come-out roll, you stop betting and wait until the shooter sevens out to bet again (this takes discipline).

3.   If the shooter throws a 4 or 10 as the point, then make *two more* bets on the don't come (in addition to the original don't pass bet). If your first don't come bet loses on a natural, don't make the second don't come bet.

4.   If the shooter throws a 5 or 9 as the point, then make only *one* more bet on the don't come.

5.   If the shooter throws a 6 or 8 as the point, then stop betting.

6.   Don't increase your bets - just bet the same all the time.

7.   Try the system with a bankroll of 20 units (if your basic bet is $5, your bankroll is $100).

8.   Use the 20 units to bet with and after every win, put the winning chips aside. After you've exhausted the 20

units, add up the winnings. If less than 20 units, take a walk. If more, pocket the excess and try again with the 20 units. Three losing bets in a row and you should also walk away and try another table.

9. Don't lay odds - keep it simple.

Don't expect to break the bank with this system. However, if you have the patience to follow it you can grind out a small but decent profit. For example, I used this simple system for a total of 4 hours on a 3 day casino visit (total of five playing sessions) and I netted a nice 30 unit profit (4 out of 5 sessions were winners). This system is very simple. Try it and you'll surprise yourself with the results.

Antimartingale Don't Pass System

My good friend and craps expert, Gil Stead, developed this simple but effective playing strategy for craps. I've modified it slightly and have had good success with it over the years. You won't win every time, but if you follow the system and quit when you're suppose to, you'll enjoy many winning sessions. The heart of the system is to bet the don't pass and lay odds on all point numbers except 6 and 8. In the case of the latter, these numbers are placed. Also, a simple antimartingale money management scheme of 1, 2, 3, 5 is used to take advantage of streaks of wins of 4 or more. The details of the system are as follows:

1. Purchase $100 in chips preferably eighteen $5 chips and ten $1 chips.

2. Make your first wager $5 on the don't pass on the come-out roll.

3. Lay odds of $9 to win $6 on the point number 5 and 9 and $10 to win $5 on the 4 or 10. Don't lay odds if a 6 or 8 is rolled.

4.   If the point is 6 or 8, make a $6 place bet on the number (6 or 8).

5.   After every winning don't pass bet, increase your wager following this progression: $5 to $10 to $15 to $25 then back to $5. Always lay single odds.

6.   Always revert back to the basic $5 bet following a loss.

7.   Don't lose more than $100 in one session.

8.   Once a shooter has made a point and/or thrown a natural 7 or 11 on the come-out, stop betting on this shooter. This will prevent you from getting wiped out on a "hot roll" by any shooter. Once the shooter sevens out and the dice pass, now you can make your basic $5 bet.

9.   You should quit a session once a profit of $50 (or more) is achieved. Stay on the table as long as possible as long as you are winning. Once the tide turns, be ready to walk. In any event, don't lose back your $50 (or more) profits.

10. You can make your starting wager more than $5. Just remember to scale your bets in the following increments: 1, 2, 3, 5. When you try this system, you'll be surprised at its simplicity and if you discipline yourself to follow the rules (especially the one that says stop betting if a shooter wins), you'll be able to enjoy many winning sessions.

Power Craps System
The following system is designed for bets on the pass line with odds and the place bets on the 6 and 8. If you remember, these bets are the best bets for the craps shooter which makes this a "powerful" system.

1.   Make the size of your pass line plus odds bet about equal to the bet on the 6 and 8. If you bet $5 on the pass line, your single odds bet would be $5 or $6 depending upon the point for a total investment of $10 or $11. Your bet on the 6 and 8 should therefore be $12 each (the $25 pass line bettor would place bet the 6 or 8 for $60 each).

2.   For the $5 bettor, a session bankroll of $350 is required to give the system a good test.

3.   Bet $5 on the pass line, take full single odds on all points and then place bet the 6 and 8 for $12 each.

4.   When a place bet wins, make your next bet on the winning number - $18. The betting progression to use on the 6 and the 8 place numbers is $12-$18-$30-$42-etc. In other words, increase your winning bet by about 50% and pocket the profit.

5.   All winning pass line bets should also be increased by 50%.

6.   Take down your place bets on the 6 or 8 if either number becomes a point. When you again make a place bet on either 6 or 8, do so with your basic $12 bet.

7.   Following any loss either on pass line or place 6 or 8, make your next bet the minimum bet ($5 for pass line, $12 for 6 and 8).

8.   If you want to make a double odds bet, then the basic $12 place 6 and 8 bet must be increased to $18 and your session bankroll should be $500.

This organized method of betting on the 6 and 8 allows you to capitalize on streaks with no limit on how much you can win. Even if you lose a bet after winning a few, the 50% progression still allows you to show a profit for that progression. Try it - and with a little luck (lots of 6's and 8's) you'll be pleasantly surprised at the system's performance.

Hedge System for 6/8

This system is designed to hedge your place bets on the 6 and 8 by making a simultaneous bet on the don't pass. It works as follows:

1.   Make your first bet on the don't pass on the come-out roll (assume $10).

2.   If a point number is rolled other than the 6 or 8, then wager $6 on the 6 and $6 on the 8.

3.   If neither the 6 or 8 is rolled on the next three rolls, then take down (remove) the two place bets on the 6 and 8.

4.   If the 6 or 8 is rolled, then take down the remaining place bet.

The strategy behind this system is to hope that the shooter throws the 6 or 8 within three rolls after making these bets. If the shooter tosses a seven, instead, you lose the two $6 place bets but you win the $10 don't pass bet. Your net loss is limited to only $2. Likewise, the system allows you to take down an immediate profit if either the 6 or 8 is rolled. The third possibility is that the shooter hasn't thrown the 6, 8 or 7 within three rolls. In this case, take down your 6 and 8 place bets, let the don't pass stay, and hope the shooter obliges with a 7. If he does, you win your don't pass bet.

This is a more conservative system than just making bets on the 6 and 8. And with a little luck, you'll be able to generate profits by hedging your place bets.

Break Even or Win System

"Is there a craps system in which you can't lose your bet once a point is established?" The answer is yes and here it is.

1. The only bets you make are on the don't pass, don't come and place bets.

2. Make your first bet on the don't pass. When a point is established, you make a place bet on the number that was established as the point.

3. Make another bet on don't come and immediately place the number that is rolled for an equal amount.

4. You should have two numbers covered. The point number is covered with the don't pass and place bet and the come number is covered with the don't come and place bet.

5. Stop betting. When you win a place bet, then make another don't come/place combo bet.

6. Continue to bet this way until the shooter sevens out.

7. Start the betting at 1 unit (eg $5) and if the shooter continues to make the numbers you are betting on, increase your bets to 2 units ($10).

Once the shooter establishes a point number, by betting in the above manner, you can't lose. For example, if you make a $5 bet on the don't pass and 4 is thrown as the point, you would immediately place the 4 for another $5. One of two events could occur. Assume the shooter makes the 4. In this case you lose your $5 don't pass bet but you win $9 on the place bet on the 4. Net win is $4. In the event the shooter sevens out, you'll lose the $5 place bet but win an equal amount on the don't pass. Net result in this case is to break out even. No matter what the point is, you always break out even if a shooter sevens out and win a little should the shooter make a number. Although the system appears to be a can't lose proposition there is one obstacle you have to overcome, namely, getting past the initial come out roll. With your bet on don't pass, you'll lose on a throw of a 7 or 11 and win on a 2 or 3. Unfortunately, the 7/11 combo is far more prevalent than the 2 or 3 so the house has the edge on the come out. But once a point is made, you are in the driver's seat.

Don't expect to make a big killing with this system. It is for conservative players only.

Don't Pass Money Management System

This system is aimed at the novice craps player. It involves making only one bet, on the don't pass, and a system for managing your money so that you don't end up a loser even after being ahead. It's also an ideal craps system for beginners. Don't let the simplicity fool you; if you follow the system and don't make any other bets, you can end up a winner on many of your craps sessions. I call this system the Don't Pass/Money Management Craps System.

1.   Whatever your session bankroll happens to be, divide it by ten to get the amount you will be wagering on the don't pass. For example, if your session bankroll is $100, your bets on the don't pass will be $10. You only make $10 bets on the don't pass line (no more or less).

2.   In the above example, put your $100 in checks (chips) in the front chip row of the craps table. All the casinos have at least two to three rows for players to put their chips. The $100 you've placed in the front row represents your starting bankroll and what we will call your betting stake.

3.   Make all of your $10 bets on the don't pass using the chips from your betting stake. Place all of your winning chips into a second chip row.

4.   Continue to use chips from the betting stake to make your bets on the don't pass. Eventually, there will not be any chips left in the betting stake (all used up in making bets). When this occurs, it is time to count your winnings in the second chip row. If your winnings exceed $100, quit the session a winner. If you have less, convert these chips into the betting stake and start the cycle again.

5.   You should quit the session when either your winnings exceed your original betting stake, or your winnings are 50% (or less) of your betting stake. Of course, if the latter occurs, you've lost 50% of what you started with.

That's all there is to this simple system. Keep betting $10 on the don't pass and use the concept of a betting stake and winnings to keep track of how much you are ahead or behind. With a little luck, you'll be able to generate some nice profits.

Place 6 and 8 Systems
This is another ideal system for beginners. It involves betting only on the 6 and 8 as follows.

1.   Wait for an eligible shooter. That is a shooter that has won by either making his/her point or throwing a natural on the come-out roll.

2.   Do not wager on pass line. Wait for the point to be established, then wager $6 each on the 6 and 8.

3.   As soon as one bet wins, take your $7 profit and tell the dealer to take down both bets.

4.   Do not bet again until a new point is established.

5.   If you win the first $7, make your next bet on 6 and 8, $6 each. If you win again (another $7), increase your bets on the next cycle to $12 each on 6 and 8. Win the $12 bet (profit of $28), then start the cycle again at $6 each on 6 and 8. Remember the next cycle starts after a new pass line point is established.

6.   Do not increase your bets following a loss. Only increase from $6 to $12 after winning two successive place bets. And always remember to wait for the eligible shooter or once a point is established to make your bets.

7.   Your bankroll should be ten times the amount of your bets. In the above case, you need a $120 bankroll. Split the bankroll into 3 sessions ($40 per session) and do not lose more than $40 per session.

8.   The system also can be applied to larger bets on 6 and 8 ($12 each). Just size your bankroll accordingly.

The goal is to win a small profit from each shooter. When it happens, take the session profits and run!

21

Dealer Tipping

Dealers often receive minimum wage and depend upon tips for their livelihood. If the dealers at your table have been friendly and helpful, I suggest making a bet(s) for them. Even if the bet(s) loses, they appreciate the gesture.

Often players make a "two way yo" or "two way hardway bet" as a way of making a bet for the dealers. The player wagers two chips instead of one on one of the prop bets. One chip represents the dealers bet; the other the player. Essentially if the player wins the bet, so do the dealers. If the bet loses, both chips go to the casino bank.

I don't like to make prop bets for dealers because of the high casino advantage. I prefer instead to make a pass line bet for them by placing a chip(s) next to my pass line bet and announce this bet is for the dealers (please don't use the term "for the boys"). I will also make an odds bet for them if a point is established.

It's not necessary to make the same size pass line bet for the dealers as for your bet. I often will make a $5 bet for the dealers once I start winning which usually means my pass line bet is larger.

Dealers provide a service and like any other person who provides a service, if you're happy with it you have the option to tip. It's your call.

22

Craps Tournaments

There are many craps tournaments offered by casinos throughout the country. Publications like "Casino Player" often list when and where these tournaments will be offered.

Tournament craps is different than the normal game since in tournaments your objective is to end up with more money (chips) than the fellow players at your table. You must therefore not only pay attention to your bankroll, but also to those of your opponents.

Every contestant in a tournament must buy-in for a fixed sum and play for a certain time period or specific number of dice rolls.

Although each tournament may vary their tournament rules, most involve playing rounds divided into elimination rounds and then the finals.

In the initial elimination rounds, all players are randomly assigned to a craps table and positions around the table. The player in position 1 bets first and other players follow in order. This order of betting occurs at the start of competition and when the dice pass to a new shooter.

Otherwise, all bets are placed in customary craps fashion.

Usually the top two (or sometimes one) table winners will advance to the next round to play other table winners. Eventually, 12 or so table winners will compete in a final championship round for the top money (prizes).

In tournament play you must stack your chips in the rails in front of you by same color (denomination) so that every player can see how much every other player has.

One advantage tournament craps offers is that a player's losses are limited to the buy-in but the sky's the limit on how much can be won. However, because the strategy in tournament craps is different, the risks are generally greater.

There is no one tried and true way to play in craps tournaments. The following is advice I can offer you based upon my experiences in tournaments and my interviews with successful tournament winners.

1.   Most casinos charge a tournament fee ($250 is normal). It's important that you ascertain how many contestants will be allowed in the tournament and what is the prize structure. What you want are tournaments that give back all the tournament entrance fees in prizes. For example, if a craps tournament has a $250 entry fee with 100 contestants, and returns the entire $25,000 ($250 x 100) in prizes, they are returning the entire equity. This would be an acceptable tournament.

2.   Always contact the casino beforehand to get a copy of their tournament rules. Here you'll find the tournament fee, prize structure, number of contestants and the required table buy-in. Some tournaments require $500 buy-ins, others $750, $1000, and more.

3.   My best successes occur when I play conservative during the round and then at the end, adjust my bets according to whether I'm ahead or behind the table leaders.

4.   If the table leader bets ahead of you, one way to catch up is to bet the opposite of the way he or she bets. Thus if the leader is betting on the pass line and making place bets, you should bet on the don't side. This way if he loses, you'll be a winner.

5.   A common tactic on the last few rolls is to make a proposition bet with high payoffs in order to catch or pass the leader. Most tournaments limit the amount you can bet on the props so check the rules. Betting on the propositions is a high risk play.

6.   Be careful of players who try to hide their chips. Tournament rules specify that each player's chips need to be grouped together in the rails by the same denomination and visible to other players. Sometimes there is a countdown toward the end where all players' chips are counted. You should still practice calculating how much a row of green or red chips is worth. You must make your best estimate how much the leader is ahead and adjust your bets accordingly.

7.   A lot of craps tournament players take a high risk, all or nothing approach. They'll make a maximum bet if necessary with all of their remaining chips in the hopes of making a score. Try to always have at least one chip left after the last betting round. I once witnessed a group of players tap out on the last roll and one of the two table winners had one red chip left.

8.   Always remember that the objective in tournament craps is to have more money at the end of the round than your fellow players. Often times, you may end up having less money than when you started but still more than anyone else.

9.   Be aware of those bets that can be removed from the table at any time. Some players make a large bet on

pass line, then take maximum odds only to remove the odds bet a few rolls later.

10. I have seen tournament players play their regular game during the whole tournament and end up a winner. They are content to bet pass line and a few comes with odds and hope that they end up ahead of the other contestants. This is a low risk approach to tournament play where the risk of losing the buy-in is very low.

Tournament craps is fun and exciting but it is also more risky than regular craps. Literally anything can happen and usually does in a tournament as most players make unorthodox plays to either keep the lead or try to catch up. There are "fun" craps tournaments in Las Vegas and Mississippi where the stakes are low. These tournaments are a good way to get some experience with a low risk.

23

The Dumb Craps Player

A typical dumb craps player - one that the casinos love to cater to - bets the following way. After getting his marker for a thousand or so dollars in chips he puts a pile of chips on the pass line. When a point is established he bets a bundle on all the numbers with a few chips tossed on the point number as a hardway bet and maybe even a two way CE bet, or if he really feels lucky another few chips on the "yo." Naturally when his number hits he instructs the dealer to press his bets. And often when things aren't going very well, he'll increase his betting limits as a way to catch up as quickly as possible. This type of player looks impressive at the craps table as he barks out instructions to the dealers and tosses chips to the stickperson almost non-stop between dice throws. Dealers cater to these players because they often tip them very well.

Sometimes, these players win big when a hot roll occurs. But more often than not, they end up big losers.

It's tempting at the craps table to toss a few $1 chips on the hardways or other prop bets. But you're a fool or absolutely crazy to do so with the astronomical casino edge these bets command.

To be a consistent winner at craps you must lay off the bets with a high casino advantage and stick to bets that have the lowest casino edge. There is *no other way* to be a winner at craps.

Smart consistent winning players do the following.

1.   They have developed a game plan before heading for their favorite casinos. This includes determining which bets they will make at what betting level, with what bankroll, and when to quit.

2.   They study up on the game of craps and know which are the best bets, the ones with the lowest casino edge.

3.   The smart player never bets more when losing, rather he bets more when winning.

4.   The smart player never limits the amount that can be won on any session - he or she never quits on a winning streak.

5.   The smart player sets a limit on the amount he or she is willing to lose at any one session.

6.   The smart player divides the bankroll into mini-session bankrolls.

7.   The smart player sets realistic win expectations.

8.   The smart player learns to take the money and run.

Don't be a dumb player; stick with the bets with the lowest casino edge with proper money management, and become a smart, winning craps player.

GLOSSARY

Here are common terms or expressions used in the game of craps.

Ace...the one spot or pip on a single die.

Ada from Decatur...Slang expression for the number 8 in craps.

Any craps...A wager on craps layout for betting that the 2, 3, 12 will be thrown on next dice toss.

Bar...The number 12 (or sometimes 2) that appear in don't pass betting area. A bar 12 means if 12 is rolled the don't pass wager is a standoff.

Bet the Dice to Win...Making a wager on the pass line.

Big Dick/Big John...Slang expression for number 10 in craps.

Big 6...A wager on craps layout for betting the 6 will be thrown before a 7.

Big 8...A wager on craps layout for betting the 8 will be thrown before a 7.

Box Cars...Slang expression for number 12 in craps (two 6's).

Boxperson...Casino supervisor that sits in front of the casino bank of every craps table. This person is the boss of that table and settles any disputes.

Buck...The marker (looks like a hockey puck) that is used to indicate the shooter's point.

Check Rack...The racks used by casinos to stack the chips at craps tables.

Cold Dice...Slang expression indicating no one is able to make a point number (i.e. pass line bettors are losing).

Come Bet...A wager on craps layout made after a point is established. Has the same win/lose rules as pass line bet.

Come Out...The initial roll of the dice by a new shooter to establish the point.

Crap Out...Slang expression indicating a shooter throws one of the craps numbers (2, 3 or 12).

Dice Stick...The curved stick used by the dealer (known as stickman or sticklady) to manipulate the dice on the table.

Deuce...Refers to the number 2 in craps.

Don't Come Bet...A wager on craps layout made after a point is established. Has the same win/lose rules as don't pass bet.

Don't Pass Line...A wager on craps layout made on a come out roll in which the player bets against the shooter. Bet wins if 2, 3 is thrown on a come out roll (12 is a standoff); loses on a natural 7 or 11. Once a point is established bet wins if 7 appears before point number, loses if point number is thrown before a 7.

Drop Box...The locked cash box located under the craps table in which the cash paid by players for chips is placed (or dropped).

Edge...An advantage in a game usually expressed as a percent. Also known as casino advantage.

Fever...Slang expression for number 5 in craps.

Field...A wager on craps layout that one of the field numbers will show on next dice toss.

Flat Bet...The initial bet on pass or don't pass.

Front Line...Another expression for pass line wager.

Hardway Bet...A wager in the center of craps table that can be made in which the player bets that either the 4, 6, 8 or 10 will be made by an identical pair of combinations on two die before rolling a 7 or the hardway number in any other combination.

Hop Bets...A one roll bet that a player can make on any number not listed on the layout.

Hot Dice...Slang expression indicating shooter is rolling a lot of numbers and making his/her points. Opposite of cold dice.

House Percentage...Another expression for edge or casino advantage.

Insurance Bet...Making a second bet to protect from losing another bet on the craps table.

Lay the Odds...Expression that indicates a player is making an odds bet on don't pass or don't come. The player wagers more to receive less (lays the odds) because once a point is established, the don't bettor has the edge.

Little Joe...Slang expression for number 4 in craps.

Long Shot Bet...Another expression for proposition bet.

Marker...Another term for buck that is used mark the shooter's point.

Natural...The numbers 7 and 11 in craps are known as naturals.

One Roll Bet...A bet in craps that is won or lost on next dice roll.

Pass...Slang expression to indicate the shooter either threw a natural on come out roll or made his or her point.

Pass Line...A wager on craps layout made on come out roll in which the player is betting with the shooter. Bet wins if a natural (7, 11) is thrown on come out roll, loses on 2, 3 or 12. Once a point is established, bet wins if point number repeats before a 7; loses if instead a 7 is rolled before point number.

Payoff...Winning chips received by a player after winning a bet.

Phoebe...Another slang expression for number 5 in craps.

Place Bet...A wager on craps layout directly on the point numbers 4, 5, 6, 8, 9, 10. Bet wins if number repeats before a 7 is rolled, loses if 7 is thrown before the number.

Point...The number (either 4, 5, 6, 8, 9, 10) rolled by a shooter on the come out roll.

Proposition Bet...A wager on one of the bets in the center of craps layout that have a high payoff.

Right Bettor...A player betting the dice to win (pass line).

Roll...The thrown of the dice by the shooter.

Seven Out...Expression indicating that the shooter threw the 7 before repeating the point number.

Shooter...Player who is throwing the dice.

Stake...The amount of money or bankroll a player has available for playing craps.

Snake Eyes...The number 2 in craps.

Stand Off...Term that indicates a player doesn't win or lose a don't pass or don't come bet when a 12 is rolled.

Stickperson...Casino dealer that uses the curved stick to retrieve the dice. This dealer also talks up the game, makes prop bets for players and pushes the dice over to the player to shoot.

Take the Odds...The odds bet made on pass line or come bet. Player wagers less to win more by taking the odds.

Trey...The number 3 in craps.

Wrong Bettor...A player betting the dice to lose (don't bettor).

SUGGESTED READING

These are my favorite books. I can recommend them to anyone who wants to learn more about craps.

All About Craps, by John Gallehon. A good beginner's guide to craps.

Winning Casino Craps, by Edwin Silberstang. Presents an excellent summary of all the bets with good playing strategies and money management.

The Dice Doctor Revised, by Sam Grafstein. I played craps with the late Sam Grafstein and he was a true master of the game. This book is a must reading for serious craps players.

Winning Craps for the Serious Player, by J. Edward Allen. Contains good strategies for beginning to intermediate players.

Beat the Craps Out of the Casinos, by Frank Scoblete. A relatively new book with a different approach to maximizing wins and minimizing losses.

A Book on Casino Craps, by C. Ionescu Tulcea. Covers not only casino craps but other dice games. Good treatment on odds and probability.

The following magazines regularly feature articles on craps.

Casino Player, 2524 Arctic Avenue, Atlantic City, NJ 08401

Casino Magazine, 115 South Fifth Street, Minneapolis, MN 55402

A complete catalog containing the above products plus hundreds of other books on gambling can be obtained from these sources (call for a free catalogue):

Gambler's Book Club, Las Vegas, 1-800-634-6243

Gambler's General Store, Las Vegas, 1-800-332-2447

INDEX

A
Antimartingale don't pass, 99
any seven, 53
any craps, 53

B
backline bet, 18
bankroll, 64
barring the 12, 15
basics, 13
beginners don't pass system, 98
betting right, 14
betting right or wrong, 74
betting wrong, 14
big 6 and 8, 47
bookkeeper, 6
boxperson, 6
break even or win system, 103
bridging, 21
buy bets, 39

C
casino advantage, 57
come out roll, 13
come bet, 25
commission, 39

contract bet, 14, 27
crapless craps, 91
craps tournaments, 109
craps 2, 53
craps 12, 53
craps 3, 53
craps numbers, 13

D
dealer tipping, 107
dealers, 5
dice, 9
dice odds, 9
don't come, 30
don't pass money management system, 104
double odds, 22, 85
dumb craps player, 103

E
eligible shooter, 53
etiquette, 12

F
field bets, 43
five time odds, 22
floorpersons, 6
fun craps tournament, 112

G
glossary, 105

H
hardway bets, 52
hedge betting, 81
hedge system for 6/8, 102
heeling, 21
horn bet, 54
horn high, 54
hot roll, 26

I
Increase Odds system, 62

L
lay bets, 41
laying odds, 20
layout, 4
live video craps, 93

M
money management, 64
multiple odds, 22
multiple odds revisited, 85

N
naturals, 13
Never Ever Craps, 79
no roll, 16
not working, 38

O

odds working, 28
odds bet, 17
off, 38
off and on, 29
on button, 28

P
pass line, 13
pit, 6
pitboss, 6
place bets, 33, 34
place 6 and 8 systems, 105
point rolls, 14
power craps system, 100
press the bet, 37
proposition bets, 51

R
removing bets, 77

S
Sam Grafstein, 76
same dice, 12
sevening out, 15
single odds, 19, 22
stickperson, 6
systems, 97

T
take down, 38
ten times odds, 22
tournament fee, 110
triple odds, 22
twenty seven across, 36
two way yo, 97

W
winning strategies, 61, 71

Y
yo-11, 54

Publications by Henry J. Tamburin

Blackjack: Take the Money and Run

Win at blackjack! This book will teach you how to walk away from the blackjack tables with profits. The winning techniques are based on Dr. Tamburin's 25 years of experience as a winning blackjack player. You'll learn the basics of how the game is played and which blackjack games offer you the most profit potential, a non-counting winning strategy for the beginner, a unique streak count betting system for the intermediate player, and a powerful advanced level system that will give you up to a 1.5% edge over the casinos. The ultimate source of blackjack winning techniques for all players who want to improve their game. $15.95

Blackjack - Deal Me in Video

Play like an expert after you view this video! Filmed in a Mississippi casino with a professional dealer, Henry Tamburin will guide you with clear explanations and demonstrations on how to play blackjack, the different rules and playing options, the basic playing strategy, and how to manage your money for maximum profits. After viewing this tape you'll know how to pick a table, how to use hand signals, how to keep more of your winnings, and when to move to another table. You'll know *exactly* when to take a hit, when to stand, when to double down, which pairs to split, and how to tip the dealer. This professionally produced, 90 minute, full color VHS video also contains graphics that highlight the strategies and a handy index that allows fast forwarding to review any topic. Makes learning how to play and win at blackjack fun and easy. $23.95

Reference Guide to Casino Gambling

This book contains the basic playing rules and winning tips for 25 of the most popular casino games offered in land and water based casinos throughout the country. Includes blackjack, craps, roulette, baccarat, video poker, big six wheels, pai gow poker, caribbean stud, slots, keno, sic bo, lowball, red dog, hold'em, draw poker, and seven card stud. An excellent one volume source for all your favorite casino games. $15.95

The Ten Best Casino Bets Second Edition

A pocket size book that explains how to make the ten most player favorable bets in a casino. Includes blackjack, craps pass/don't pass with odds, baccarat bank and player bets, craps place bets on 6 and 8, video poker, craps lay bet on 4 and 10, pai gow poker, and roulette. Also contains chapters on betting strategies, money management, and the psychology of gambling. Great book for the novice to intermediate player. $5.00

Winning Baccarat Strategies

This classic book contains effective card counting systems for the casino game of baccarat. You'll learn how the game is played, a simple running count system, the true count system, how to put the count to work, money management concepts, and ESP and baccarat. The counting strategies are based on three years of intensive research and the computer analysis of more than *175 million games*. Even if you've never played baccarat, this book will quickly teach you the strategies and techniques for winning play. $20.00

Pocket Blackjack Strategy Card

A durable, plastic coated, hand held pocket card that contains the complete blackjack playing strategy. Take it with you to the tables and refer to it. You will never make a costly playing mistake! Casino legal. Makes *any* player a *skillful* player. $3.00

To order any of the above, send name and address with check or money order to:

Research Services Unlimited
P.O. Box 19727
Greensboro, NC 27419

(The above prices include shipping and handling)

For VISA/MC orders call toll free

1-888-353-3234

About the Author

Henry Tamburin has been actively involved in casino gambling for the past 25 years as a player, author, instructor, and columnist. He has operated a casino gambling school to teach winning techniques to the public, written and published a newsletter on Atlantic City casino gambling and operated a club for casino players. He also writes a weekly newspaper column on casino gambling and authored many articles that have appeared in every major gaming magazine. His "how to win" seminars are well received by clubs/organizations. Henry has appeared on TV and radio and his exploits as a winning casino player and public educator have been featured in several newspaper stories. Most recently he is featured in the new instructional videos *Blackjack - Deal Me In* and *Craps - Rolling To Win*.

His books include: *Blackjack: Take the Money and Run, Reference Guide to Casino Gambling, The Ten Best Casino Bets Second Edition, Winning Baccarat Strategies, WBS Chart Book, Henry Tamburin on Casino Gambling, Casino Gambler's Survival Book, Casino Gambler's Quiz Book,* and *Pocket Reference to Casino Gambling*.

Henry Tamburin is a graduate of Seton Hall University with a Bachelor of Science degree in Chemistry, and the University of Maryland with a Doctor of Philosophy degree in Organic Chemistry. He works for a large international chemical company in research and development and production management. He and his wife Linda have two grown sons.